Arabs Speak Frankly

on the

Arab-Israeli Conflict

With original documents

and

comments by world leaders

and writers

Compiled by Naomi Comay

Published in Great Britain by
Printing Miracles Limited
2005

ISBN 0-9550312-0-6

Printed and bound in Great Britian by
Cromwell Press, Wiltshire

Foreword

Arabs Speak Frankly is a well overdue book that is badly needed to not only show that there are Arabs who support the democratic Israel but to counter balance many of the distortions apparent in the Western media. I am happy both to endorse the contents of this book as well as participate in the dialogue.

Walid Shoebat
Former PLO terrorist
22nd November 2004

Introduction

Many modern historians hold the view that history is a matter of interpretation, that it is written by the "winner", that statements by participants in an event are not reliable, and that there are no "empirical facts".

This book takes the opposite view. It relies on statements made at the time by eye witnesses and those who were involved in what happened, rather than on interpretations written decades later. Each section consists of quotations from Arabs and concludes with comments by contemporary world leaders and journalists. With only two exceptions, none are from Jews, and yet the story which emerges is not the one which usually comes from the Arab world.

The sources of all the quotations, and where possible their translators, are listed and are easily verifiable. Where the sources were not available, quotations were reluctantly omitted.

Many of the final quotations and comments suggest cautious hope that there can finally be an end to the hundred year-old conflict.

In a talk to the Conservative Foreign and Commonwealth Council on 1/2/05, the Arab League Ambassador to Britain said "We would like you to read about our state of affairs through what we write ourselves, not through what others write about us" *.

This book endeavours to do just that.

Ain Al-Yaqeen, Saudi Royal Family weekly online magazine, 1/4/05 (www.memri.org) and (www.cfconline.org.uk)

Contents

Maps

Appendix

1.

Pre-Mandate

This short section on Palestine during the Ottomann rule has been included as a background to subsequent events. The following quotations are from visitors to the area.

WORLD VIEWS

"The country is in a considerable degree empty of inhabitants and therefore its greatest need is of a body of population".

James Finn, British Consul, 1857
(www.palestinefacts.org)

"We never saw a human being on the whole route [Palestine]....Bethlehem and Bethany .... untenanted by any living creature .... There is not a solitary village throughout its whole extent [Valley of Jezreel]".

Mark Twain, "The Innocents Abroad", 1867
(www.palestinefacts.org)

"The road leading from Gaza to the north was only a summer track...no orange groves, orchards or vineyards until one reached the Jewish village of Yavneh".

Palestine Royal Commission, 1913
("Myths and Facts 1976", Near East Report, Washington, 1976)

Sykes-Picot Agreement 1916

(Division of territory between France and Great Britain, on defeat of Turkish Empire in World War I)

"It is accordingly understood between the French and British governments:

That France and Great Britain are prepared to recognize and protect an independent Arab state or a confederation of Arab states (a) and (b) marked on the annexed map, under the suzerainty of an Arab chief. That in area (a) France, and in area (b) great Britain, shall have priority of right of enterprise and local loans. That in area (a) France, and in area (b) great Britain, shall alone supply advisers or foreign functionaries at the request of the Arab state or confederation of Arab states.

That in the blue area France, and in the red area Great Britain, shall be allowed to establish such direct or indirect administration or control as they desire and as they may think fit to arrange with the Arab state or confederation of Arab states".

www.yale.edu/lawweb

Sykes-Picot Agreement

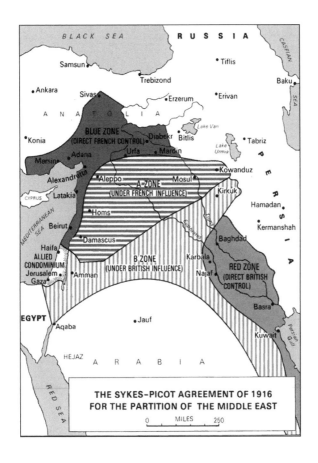

A History of Israel, Knopf, 1979 (www.us-israel.org)

4   Arabs Speak Frankly

2.

British Mandate

Original Area of British Mandate to which
Balfour Declaration applied

"Christians, Israel, and the Struggle for Peace",
Christian Friends of Israel, September 2003:
www.cfi.org.uk

WORLD VIEWS

"Small in area - comparable in size to Belgium or Wales....The country was before the War, and is now, undeveloped and under-populated....under-populated because of this lack of development. There are now in the whole of Palestine hardly 700,000 people....four-fifths...are Muslims.

After the persecutions in Russia forty years ago, the movement of the Jews to Palestine assumed larger proportions. Jewish agricultural colonies were founded. They developed the culture of oranges and gave importance to the Jaffa orange trade. They cultivated the vine, and manufactured and exported wine. They drained swamps. They planted eucalyptus trees. They practiced, with modern methods, all the processes of agriculture.

"The wildest stories as to the intentions of the Jews and the fate awaiting the Arabs were circulated in the towns and villages, and were often believed by a credulous people. Among a section of the Arabs, who had all previously lived on excellent terms with the Jewish population, a bitter feeling was evoked against the Jews. It was fostered and developed until it culminated in a serious outbreak in the streets of Jerusalem in April 1920, when a number of Jews were killed and wounded and Jewish shops were looted....Many men of education among the Arabs took no part, however, in this antagonism. They recognised that the fears that had been expressed were illusory. They realised that Jewish co-operation was the best means, perhaps the only means, of promoting the prosperity of Palestine, a prosperity from which the Arabs could not fail to benefit".

Interim Report to the League of Nations by
Herbert Samuel, High Commissioner of the
British Mandate in Palestine, 30/7/21

3.
Balfour Declaration 1917 *

"His Majesty's Government view with favour the establishment in Palestine of a national home for the Jewish people, and will use their best endeavours to facilitate the achievement of the object".

Arthur James Balfour, Foreign Office, UK, November 1917
("Myths and Facts 1976", Near East Report, Washington, 1976)
*For full text see Appendix A

"Recognition has thereby been given to the historical connection of the Jewish people with Palestine and to the grounds for reconstructing their national home".

League of Nations endorsement of Balfour Declaration and
British Mandate for Palestine, 12/8/22
(www.iacnet.org)

"The Mandatory shall be responsible for placing the country under such administrative and economic conditions as will secure the establishment of the Jewish national home".

San Remo Conference, endorsement of
British Mandate for Palestine, 1922
(www. geocities.com)

"The Arabs, especially the educated among us, look with deepest sympathy on the Zionist movement....We will wish the Jews a hearty welcome home....We are working together for a reformed and revived Near East and our two movements complete one another.   The Jewish movement is nationalist and not imperialist.   Our movement is nationalist and not imperialist. And there is room in Syria for us both. *[Under Turkish rule, Syria included part of Palestine]* Indeed, I think that neither can be a real success without the other".

Emir Faisal, son of acknowledged leader of the Arabs, Sherif Hussein, in a letter to Felix Frankfurther, 3/3/1919 ("Myths and Facts 1976", Near East Report, Washington, 1976)

Partition, allocating 80% of promised British Mandate to an Arab State, 1922

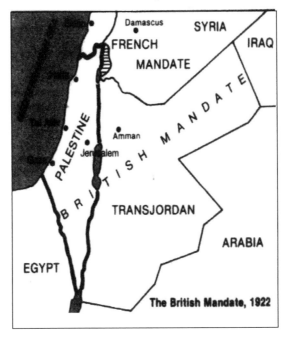

Ceded to the French Mandate of Syria in 1923

"Christians, Israel, and the Struggle for Peace",
Christian Friends of Israel,
September 2003: www.cfi.org.uk)

For full text of approval of British Mandate by
League of Nations, see Appendix B

4.
Peel Plan for Partition
of Palestine 1937

[Rejected by Arab world]
Peel Commission, Royal Commission Report

Partition Plan, 1937, London HMSO

"The primary purpose of the mandate...is to promote the establishment of the Jewish National Home".

www.domino.un.org

WORLD VIEW

"So far from persecuted, the Arabs have crowded into the country and multiplied till their population has increased more than even all world Jewry could lift up the Jewish population".

Winston Churchill, 1939,
(www.geocities.com)

5.
UN Partition Plan 1947

The UN Partition Plan, 1947.

"Myths and Facts 1976",
Near East Report, Washington, 1976

UN Resolution 181 *

"Independent Arab and Jewish States and the Special International Regime for the City of Jerusalem...shall come into existence in Palestine two months after the armed forces of the mandatory power has been completed but in any case not later than 1 October 1948". [rejected by the Arab States]

UN Resolution 181, 29/11/47,
(United Nations: www.domino-un.org)
* For full text see Appendix C

6.
War 1948

"The representatives of the Jewish Agency told us yesterday that they were not the attackers, that the Arabs had begun the fighting. We did not deny this. We told the whole world that we were going to fight".

Jamal Husseini, to the UN Security Council, 1948
("Myths and Facts 1976", Near East Report, Washington, 1976)

"When the state of Israel was established, Arab countries participated in a military effort to end the presence of the Jewish state in Palestine".

Mustafa Kamal Said, professor of political science and director of the Centre of Developing Countries at Cairo University, in an Interview with Bitterlemons, February 2003
(www.bitterlemons-international.org)

"On the night of April 9th, the peaceful Arab village of Deir Yassin was surprised by a loudspeaker, which called on the population to evacuate it immediately".

"Israeli Agression", Arab League publication,
(www.etzel.org.il, 28/5/04)

"I asked Dr Khalid [secretary of the Arab Higher Committee] how we should cover the story. He said 'We must make the most of this'. So we wrote a press release stating that at Deir Yassin children were murdered, pregnant women were raped. All sorts of atrocities".

Hazen Nusseibeh, an editor of the Palestine
Broadcasting Service's Arabic News in 1948,
in an interview for BBC TV series
"Israel and the Arabs: the 50-year conflict", (1998)

"There were no rapes. It's all lies. There were no pregnant women who were split open. It was propaganda that... Arabs put out so Arab armies would invade. They ended up expelling people from all of Palestine on the rumour of Deir Yassin".

Muhammed Radwan, Deir Yassin survivor and fighter, quoted
in an article "Deir Yassin, a casualty of guns and
propaganda" by Paul Holmes, Reuters, 20/4/88,
(www.metimes.com/issue98-16/reg/deir.html)

"The Jews never intended to hurt the population of the village, but were forced to do so after they met enemy fire".

Yunes Ahmad Assad,
prominent Arab survivor, Al Urdan, 9/4/55
("Myths and Facts 1976", Near East Report, Washington, 1976)

"Let me state this plainly and clearly: the Jews in Israel took no one's land".

Joseph Farah, Arab-American journalist, 23/4/02
(www.worldnetdaily.com)

WORLD VIEWS

"The future of the Arabs of Palestine was sacrificed to Egyptian politics....The Arab governments were largely responsible for the ruin of the Palestine Arabs. By raising the hopes of the latter, they made them intransigent".

Sir John Bagot Glubb (Glubb Pasha),
"A Soldier with the Arabs" 1948
("Myths and Facts 1976", Near East Report, Washington, 1976)

"From the first week of December 1947, disorder in Palestine had begun to mount. The Arabs repeatedly had asserted that they would resist partition by force. They seemed to be determined to drive that point home by assaults upon the Jewish community in Palestine".

Trygve Lie, UN Secretary-General, "The Cause of
Peace: Seven years with the United Nations",
MacMillan, New York, 1954

"This is not the first time that the Arab states, which organised the invasion of Palestine, have ignored a decision of the Security Council or of the General Assembly. The USSR delegation deems it essential that the Council should state its opinion more clearly and more firmly with regard to this attitude of the Arab states towards decisions of the Security Council".

Andrei Gromyko, to Security Council, 28/5/48
("Myths and Facts 1976", Near East Report, Washington, 1976)

Israel's Proclamation of Independence

"In the midst of wanton aggression, we yet call upon the Arab inhabitants of the State of Israel to return to the ways of peace and to play their part in the development of the State, with full and equal citizenship and due representation in all its bodies and institutions, provisional or permanent".

Israel's Proclamation of Independence, 14/5/48
(www.yahoodi.com)

Five Arab Armies' Attack on Israel, and Israel's Repulsion of them, 1947-8

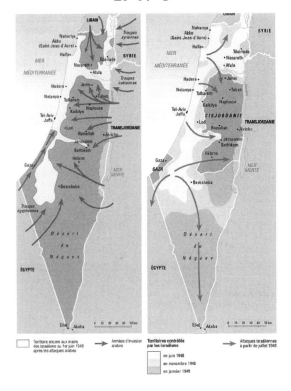

Le Monde Diplomatique, Paris (www.mondediplo.com)

Armistice Lines 1949
("Green Line")

[Israel now on 17.5% of British Mandate Territory]

("Myths and Facts 1976",
Near East Report, Washington, 1976

7.

Refugees

"A just settlement of the refugee problem".

UN Resolution 194, United Nations,
*(www.domino-un.org) ** *

"Agreement by negotiations conducted either with the Conciliation Commission or directly, with a view to the final settlement of all questions outstanding between them".

UN Resolution 194, Para 5, 11/12/48, United Nations
(www.domino-un.org)

[Superceded by Security Council Resolution 242, and non-binding as it is a General Assembly Resolution]
*** For full text see Appendix D*

"Since any solution of the refugee problem would involve important commitments by Israel, she could not be expected to make them unless at the same time, she received reasonable   assurances from her neighbours as to her national and economic security".

Palestine Conciliation Commission (PCC), 1951
(www.domino-un.org)

"The Arabs would not submit to a truce but they rather preferred to leave their homes in the town...and leave the town, which they did".

Jamal Husseini spokesman for the Arab Higher Committee, to UN Security Council, 23/4/48 ("Myths and Facts 1976", Near East Report, Washington, 1976)

"The lives of a million Jews in Moslem countries will be jeopardized by the establishment of the Jewish state".

Arab leaders, to UN debates, 1948, ("Myths and Facts 1976", Near East Report, Washington, 1976)

"The Arab armies entered Palestine to protect the Palestinians...but, instead, they abandoned them, forced them to emigrate and to leave their homeland, imposed upon them a political and ideological blockade and threw them into prisons similar to the ghettos in which the Jews used to live in Europe".

Abu Mazen, member of the PLO, in "al-Thaura" (official publication of the PLO, March 1976) (www.aish.com)

"The fact that there are these refugees is the direct consequence of the action of the Arab states in opposing partition and the Jewish state".

Emil Khoury, Secretary General of the Arab Higher Committee, September 1948 (www.pnews.org)

"The Arab High Command asked us to leave the country for two weeks to make the battle easier for them. They told us: 'A cannon cannot differentiate between a Jew and an Arab. Leave the country for two weeks, and you will come back victorious'.   I heard the Haganah microphones asked the Arabs to remain and live peacefully with their Jewish brethren".

Salim Joubran, an Arab citizen of Israel,
to American audiences, February 1962
("Myths and Facts 1976", Near East Report, Washington, 1976)

"It is shameful that the Arab governments should prevent the Arab refugees from working in their countries and shut the doors in their faces and imprison them in camps".

Musa Al-Alami, "The Lesson of Palestine",
Middle East Journal, October 1949, p.386
(www.emory.edu)

"The Arab nations keep the Palestinians and their descendants in squalor. They are denied citizenship rights. They are denied work. They are denied property. They are denied their human rights because they are and always will be a political football in the Arab campaign against Israel".

Joseph Farah, Arab-American journalist,
January 2004
(www.worldnetdaily.com)

"Ask yourself why Jordan, Egypt or Syria didn't give the Palestinians a country when they had our land. Why didn't they give Jerusalem to the Palestinians and why do they expect more of Israel?....The Arab world that has taught the Palestinians to fight. That same Arab world will not give a Palestinian citizenship....Why can't they give them equal rights? Why can't they go to schools for free?....The Palestinian refugees get aid from all over the world and yet, they don't seem to have better living conditions. The 'hosting' governments siphon off some money into its' pockets and the Palestinian authority, or lack of it, siphons off the rest and as a result the poor deserving people get nothing....To the Arab and Islamic governments, fix your own problems. Do not use our misery to blind your subjects to what is really wrong with your countries".

Sarah Elshazly, Israeli Arab
(www.arabsforisrael.com, 18/12/04)

WORLD VIEW

UN Resolution 237 "...might properly be interpreted as having application to the treatment, at the time of the recent war and as a result of that war, of both Arab and Jewish persons in the States which are directly concerned because of their participation in that war".

Nils-Goran Gussing, special representative of
Secretary General U-Thant, 1967, United Nations
(www.domino-un.org)

"The Jews have been making extensive efforts to prevent wholesale evacuation, but their propaganda appears to have had very little effect".

A British Military Observer, 8/5/48
("Myths and Facts 1976", Near East Report, Washington, 1976)

"Every effort is being made by the Jews to persuade the Arab populace to stay and carry on with their normal lives, to get their shops and businesses open and to be assured that their lives and interests will be safe".

British police report, 26/4/48
("Myths and Facts 1976", Near East Report, Washington, 1976)

"Villages were frequently abandoned even before they were threatened by the progress of war".

Glubb Pasha, former commander of the Arab Legion,
London Daily Mail, 12/9/48,
("Myths and Facts 1976", Near East Report, Washington, 1976)

"Various factors influenced their [Haifa inhabitants'] decision to seek safety in flight. There is but little doubt that the most potent of the factors were the announcements made over the air by the Arab Higher Executive, urging all Arabs in Haifa to quit. The reason given was that upon the final withdrawal of the British, the combined armies of the Arab states would invade Palestine and 'drive the Jews into the sea', and it was clearly intimated that those Arabs who remained in Haifa and accepted Jewish protection would be regarded as renegades".

British eyewitness, Economist, London, 2/10/48
("Myths and Facts 1976", Near East Report, Washington, 1976)

"As early as the first months of 1948 the Arab League issued orders exhorting the people to seek temporary refuge in neighbouring countries, later to return to their abodes in the wake of the victorious Arab armies, and obtain their share of abandoned Jewish property".

Research Group for European Migration Problems,
Bulletin, January-March 1957
("Myths and Facts 1976", Near East Report, Washington, 1976)

"The Arab States do not want to solve the refugee problem. They want to keep it as an open sore, as an affront to the United Nations and as a weapon against Israel. Arab leaders don't give a damn whether the refugees live or die".

Ralph Galloway, former director of UNRWA, August 1958
(www.camera.org)

8.

Six Day War 1967

[Seven Arab Armies Threatened Israel 1967]

"All Egypt is now prepared to plunge into total war which will put an end to Israel".

Cairo Radio's "Voice of the Arabs", 17/5/67
("Myths and Facts 1976", Near East Report, Washington, 1976)

"As of today, there no longer exists an international emergency force to protect   Israel....We shall exercise patience no more.   We shall not complain any more to the UN about Israel. The sole method we shall apply against Israel is total war which will result in the extermination of Zionist existence".

Cairo Radio's "Voice of the Arabs", 18/5/67
("Myths and Facts 1976", Near East Report, Washington, 1976)

"...keep sending commandos into Israel".

PLO, led by Arafat, reported by New York Times, 17/5/67

"Our forces are now entirely ready not only to repulse the aggression, but to initiate the act of liberation itself, and to explode the Zionist presence in the Arab homeland. The Syrian army, with its finger on the trigger is united... I as a military man, believe that the time has come to enter into the battle of liberation".

Hafez Assad, Syria's Defence Minister, 20/5/67
("Myths and Facts 1976", Near East Report, Washington, 1976)

"The Israeli flag shall not go through the Gulf of Aqaba. Our sovereignty over the entrance to the Gulf cannot be disputed".

Abdul Nasser, President of Egypt, to Egyptian army, 22/5/67 ("Myths and Facts 1976", Near East Report, Washington, 1976)

"Our basic objective will be the destruction of Israel".

Abdul Nasser, President of Egypt, May 1967 ("Myths and Facts 1976", Near East Report, Washington, 1976)

"We will not accept any...co-existence with Israel ....Today the issue is not the establishment of peace between the Arab states and Israel....The war with Israel is in effect since 1948".

Abdul Nasser, President of Egypt, 28/5/67 ("Myths and Facts 1976", Near East Report, Washington, 1976)

"The armies of Egypt, Jordan, Syria and Lebanon are poised on the borders of Israel....to face the challenge, while standing behind us are the armies of Iraq, Algeria, Kuwait, Sudan and the whole Arab nation. This act will astound the world. Today they will know that the Arabs are arranged for battle, the critical hour has arrived. We have reached the stage of serious action and not declarations".   *Abdul Nasser, President of Egypt, 30/5/67 ("Myths and Facts 1976", Near East Report, Washington, 1976)*

"Our goal is clear - to wipe Israel off the map".

President Aref of Iraq, 31/5/67 ("Myths and Facts 1976", Near East Report, Washington, 1976)

Israel after 1967 War

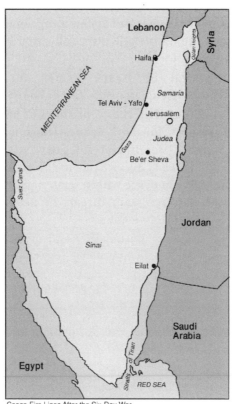

Cease-Fire Lines After the Six-Day War

www.cfi-usa.org/maps/html

UN Resolution 242 *

"The fulfilment of the Charter principles requires the establishment of a just and lasting peace in the Middle East which should include the application of both the following principles:
(i)   Withdrawal of Israeli armed forces from territories occupied in the recent conflict;
(ii)   Termination of all claims or states of belligerency and respect for and acknowledgement of the sovereignty, territorial integrity and political independence of every State in the area and their right to live in peace within secure and recognised boundaries free from threats or acts of force".
[Rejected by the Arab states.]

UN Security Council Resolution 242, 22/11/67,
United Nations   (www.domino-un.org)

*   *For full text see Appendix G*

"No peace with Israel, no recognition of Israel, no negotiations with Israel".

Arab League Summit Conference, Khartoum, November 1967,
on suggestions that they negotiate land for peace after Israel's
successful victory over the seven invading Arab armies
(www.hashd.org)

For full text see Appendix F

WORLD VIEWS

"Part of these territories can remain in Israeli hands".

Soviet delegate at UN Security Council, November 1967

"It would have been wrong to demand that Israel return to its positions of June 4th, 1967, because those positions were undesirable and artificial".

Lord Caradon, Beirut Daily Star, 12/6/74

9.

Yom Kippur War 6/10/1973

"Arab policy at this stage has but two objectives. The first, the elimination of the traces of the 1967 aggression through an Israeli withdrawal from all the territories it occupied that year. The second objective is the elimination of the traces of the 1948 aggression, by means of the elimination of the State of Israel itself".

Mohammed Heikai, editor, semi-official Al Ahram, 25/2/71
("Myths and Facts 1976", Near East Report, Washington, 1976)

"Our forces continue to pressure the enemy and will continue to strike him until we recover the occupied territory, and we will then continue until all the land [Palestine] is liberated".

Hafez Assad, Radio Damascus, 16/10/73
("Myths and Facts 1976", Near East Report, Washington, 1976)

Israel-Syria
Cease Fire Lines after 1973

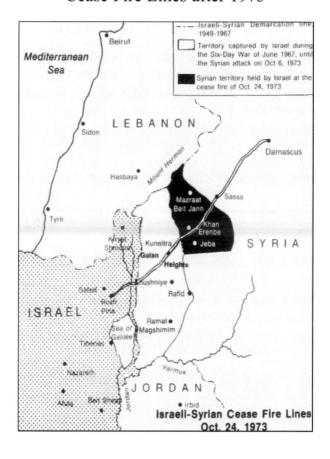

"Myths and Facts 1976",
Near East Report, Washington, 1976

Israel-Egypt
Cease Fire Lines after 1973

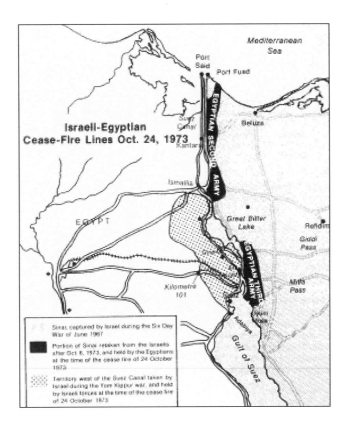

"Myths and Facts 1976",
Near East Report, Washington, 1976

10.

The Camp David Accords
17/9/1978

"The parties are determined to reach a just, comprehensive, and durable settlement of the Middle East conflict through the conclusion of peace treaties based on Security Council resolutions 242 and 338* in all their parts....

Between three months and nine months after the signing of the peace treaty, all Israeli forces will withdraw east of a line extending from a point east of El-Arish to Ras Muhammad, the exact location of this line to be determined by mutual agreement".

Framework for Peace in the Middle East, signed by Anwar Al-Sadat, President of Arab Republic of Egypt, Menachem Begin, Prime Minister of Israel, and Jimmy Carter, President of the U.S.A.
("Myths and Facts 1976", Near East Report, Washington, 1976)

*For full text see Appendix I

11.

Oslo Peace Process

Declaration of Principles 1993

"The Government of the State of Israel and the PLO team...representing the Palestinian people, agree that it is time to put an end to decades of confrontation and conflict, recognise their mutual legitimate and political rights".

13/9/93, United Nations (www.domino-un.org)
For full text see Appendix J

12.

Camp David II, 2000

[As no agreement was reached,
the negotiations continued at Taba]

Taba 2001

"The two sides agreed that in accordance with UN Security Council Resolution 242, the June 4 1967 lines would be the basis for the borders between Israel and the state of Palestine [editor's emphasis]".

"....Both sides agreed that Israeli and Palestinian areas will have sovereign contiguity".

"...Both sides agreed that there is going to be a safe passage from the north of Gaza (Beit Hanun) to the Hebron district, and that the West Bank and the Gaza must be territorially linked".

Palestinian Ministry of Foreign Affairs (www.mopic.gov.ps)

"...Both sides were prepared to commit themselves to promoting security and fighting terror".

"The Israelis sketched a map presenting a 6 percent annexation....The Palestine illustrative map presented 3.1 percent in the context of a land swap....The Israeli side adhered to a maximum 3 percent land swap as per Clinton proposal".

EU envoy Miguel Moratinos' account of Taba talks, 2002
((Palestinian Ministry of Foreign Affairs: www.mopic.gov.ps)

[The Palestinian delegation withdrew again
before an agreement was reached]

"When the peace talks between Barak, Arafat and Clinton failed, the true intention of the Palestinian leadership and its supporters, the Arab world that is keeping it alive became very clear. They don't want peace and they don't want to co-exist with Israel".

Nonie Darwish, Muslim American
who grew up in the Middle East
(www.arabsforisrael.com, 15/10/01)

"Had the Arabs accepted an agreement with Israel three years ago, they would have saved 1500 Palestinian lives, and prevented the building of the fence".

Abed El Rahman Rashid,
(editorial, London-based Arab language daily,
Al Sharq Al Awsat, 12/12/03)

Taba 2001 -
Israel's Offer of 95% Withdrawal

Final Status Map Presented by Israel - Taba, January 2001
Based on a 5% West Bank Territorial Transfer to Israel

www.fmep.org

WORLD VIEWS

"The Palestinian Authority responded by unleashing radical Islamic and nationalist militias in a purported 'war of liberation' to end the very 'occupation' Israel had just demonstrated it was willing to terminate peacefully".

International Christian Embassy Jerusalem,
5/12/2001
(www.icej.org)

"Peace talks at Camp David, and Taba ran into the sand because Arafat chose not to accept what had been negotiated but preferred to see what more could be extracted through the violence of the second intifada."

Michael Gove, The Times, 9/11/04

13.
"Intifada" 2000

"We will put Israel into the sea. There is no compromise. Co-existence is all nonsense".

Professor Adal Sadeq, Ein Shams University, Cairo,
on Iqran TV, Saudi Arabia, 2000
(Middle East Media Research Institute: www.memri.org)

"The failure *[of the Camp David Summit]* heralds the end of the political accord, and this end opens the option of struggle and violent confrontation".

Capt. Kayid Muhammad Jerada, a political guidance
agent in the National Security Border Guard,
Al-Shahada, issue no. 28, July 2000
(www.jafi.org.il)

"It would be a mistake to think that the Intifada broke out because of Ariel Sharon's visit to the Temple Mount in September 2000. It was planned after Arafat's return from Camp David, when he rejected Clinton's proposals. The PLO revived the military operations in order to escalate the fighting against Israel".

Imad Faluji, Palestinian Minister of Posts
and Communications, Al-Safir, 3/3/01
(www.memri.org)

"In order to make progress in the negotiations, confrontation is necessary".

Falastin al-Yawm, issue no. 30, 5/8/2000
Palestinian weekly, published by
Political Guidance Office responsible to Arafat.

"We will continue to aspire to the strategic goal, namely, a Palestine from the river to the sea. Whatever we get now cannot make us forget this supreme truth".

Faisal Al-Husseini, PA Minister of Jerusalem Affairs,
to a forum of Arab lawyers in Beirut 21/3/2001
(Middle East Media Research Institute: www.memr.org)

"I knew that the end of September was the last period (of time) before the explosion, but when Sharon reached the al-Aqsa Mosque, this was the most appropriate moment for the outbreak of the intifada....The night prior to Sharon's visit, I participated in a panel on a local television station and I seized the opportunity to call on the public to go to the Al-Aqsa mosque in the morning, for it was not possible that Sharon would reach al-Haram Al-Sharif just so, and walk away peacefully. I finished and went to al-Aqsa in the morning....We tried to create clashes without success because of the differences of opinion that emerged with others in the al-Aqsa compound at the time....After Sharon left, I remained for two hours in the presence of other people. We discussed the manner of response and how it was possible to react in all the cities and not just in Jerusalem. We contacted all (the Palestinian) factions".

Marwan Barghouti, interview with the London-based
Arabic daily Al-Hayat, 29/9/01, (www.jcpa.org)

"Stop murdering Israelis until we have an independent Palestinian state".

Abu Mazen, Prime Minister,
Palestinian Authority, February 2003,
(Middle East Media Research Institute: www.memr.org)

"The attitude of Islam is not to accept a foreign state in this area".

Mahmoud Zahar, Hamas spokesman, 2003
(www.news.bbc.co.uk)

"I swear by almighty God, we will not leave a single Jew in Palestine".

Abdel Aziz Rantizi, Hamas leader, June 2003
(www.seacoastonline.org)

"We have to destroy their economy, they should feel that they are insecure, we want them to leave the country".

Farouq Qaddumi, highest ranking Palestinian official
at the Organisation of the Islamic Conference
(of 57 Islamic states), Putrajaya, Malaysia, 2003
(Independent Media Review analysis: www.imra.org.il)

To the question: "If Israel accepts your conditions which are calling for the elimination of the occupation and an end for the Palestinian suffering, will you renounce violence totally?", Dr Zahar, senior spokesman for Hamas replied: "We are going to ceasefire, and only cease-fire".

Interview with Tim Sebastian, for BBC's
Hardtalk TV rogramme 20/5/03 (www.bbc.co.uk)

Violence has been "detrimental to our national struggle".

Mohammed Dahlan,
former PA Security Chief, September 2003
(Associated Press: www.ap.org)

Martyrdom "is not a question of frustration by the one martyring himself. To the contrary, this is a planned deed by means of which the martyr wishes to gain paradise".

Dr Sheikh Ali Gum'a, new Egyptian Mufti, 8/7/03
(Middle East Media Research Institute: www.memri.org)

"Senseless Violence, Senseless Death".

Dr. Muhammad Talal Al-Rasheed,
columnist, The Saudi Gazette,English language daily, 30/11/03
(www..hvk.org)

"What will it take for Israelis and Americans to understand you can't negotiate with terrorists? How much innocent blood needs to be spilled before we acknowledge the 'peace process' has failed?".

Joseph Farah, Arab-American journalist, 21/9/03
(www.worldnetdaily.com)

"The religious discourse brainwashing people day and night on the government [and] public...satellite [television] channels is a blatant expression of the backward mentality that does not believe in the other and refuses to coexist with him".

Abu Ahmad Mustafa, Arab diplomat, in London
Arabic-language daily Al-Sharq Al-Awsat, 13/9/03,
(Middle East Media Research Institute: www.memri.org)

"We must admit that those who pushed children into the second 'Intifada' did not have a definite political objective that would benefit the Palestinian people".

Abu Ahmad Mustafa, Arab diplomat, in
London
Arabic-language daily Al-Sharq Al-Awsat, May-Sept 2003,
(Middle East Media Research Institute: www.memri.org)

"Our position is clear: all of Palestine. Every inch of Palestine belongs to the Muslims. Some marginal elements in the Palestinian Authority have begun trading with the Palestinian cause as they did in Oslo".

Mahmoud Zahar, Hamas leader 13/11/03
reported by Khaled Toameh in Jerusaelm Post 14/11/03
(www.unitedjerusalem.org)

"Of course I'm angry at her *[the bomber]*. This is not only the place where we work, but our home...Whoever ordered the bombing must have known that 30,000 mouths depend on our employment here. After all, this hurts us *[the Palestinians]* much more than it does the Israelis".

Ashur Salha, Palestinian factory owner at Erez crossing point
(The Jerusalem Post, 15/1/04)

"We can talk about the rights and wrongs of the situation, but believe me: without fundamentalist Islam, nothing happening in Palestine would ever lead a 16-year-old kid to blow himself up".

"There is no solution except a military one: the crushing defeat of all Palestinian military groups, and then the imposition of a new system".

"[They] are not interested in achieving peace with Israel....They cannot be negotiated with. They have to be defeated".

Walid Shoebat, former PLO terrorist,
Sunday Telegraph, 20/6/04

"I think now that the Intifada in its entirety was a mistake, and it should not have continued, and in particular what is called 'the militarization of the Intifada".

Mahmoud Abbas (Abu Mazen), former PA Prime Minister,
interviewed by Al-Rai, Jordanian daily newspaper, 27/9/04
(www.memri.org)

"These rockets which harm Israelis in Sderot and in other places - and I am sorry for the Israeli losses - are only bringing back misery and a lot of suffering for a lot of innocent people... because they are helpless and cannot prevent the young men from launching these useless rockets....The launching of these rockets is an irresponsible act of a bunch of hotheaded young militants who are following the orders of totally irresponsible leaders of militant factions".

Samir Rantissi, Advisor to the Palestinian Authority,
in interview with IMRA, October 2004
(www.imra.org.il)

WORLD VIEWS

"There is simply no evidence of a massacre *[in Jenin]*".

Peter Bouckaert, senior researcher,
Human Rights Watch, Jenin
(The Jerusalem Post, 28/4/02)

...did not see "any evidence of a massacre. The Israeli army was fighting against some desperate (Palestinian) fighters here".

Major David Holley,
British military adviser to Amnesty International,
interview with Agence France-Presse, 28/4/02
(www.townhall.com)

"Palestinian armed groups, for their part, openly proclaim their determination to kill Israeli civilians. Suicide bombings and other attacks on buses and other public places carried out by Palestinian groups, including the armed wing of Hamas, Islamic Jihad, and Al-Aksa Martyrs Brigades, deliberately aim to kill as many Israeli civilians as possible".

Amnesty International 30/9/03,
on 3rd anniversary of the intifada,
(ngo monitor analysis, www.iacnet.org)

"The bombings ... are deplorable, they represent a path to violence, they are certainly contrary to the interests of peace".

Brian Cowen, Irish Foreign Minister
(The Jerusalem Report, 29/01/04: www.jrep.com)

The deliberate targeting of civilians is a heinous crime and cannot be justified by any cause. We urge the PA to take the steps necessary to bring to justice those who plan, facilitate and carry out such crimes".

Kofi Annan, UN Press release, 23/11/02
(www.mideasttruth.com)

"Sometimes I am not sure that everyone living outside of Israel today fully comprehends the situation on the ground. I am not sure that every outside observer fully understands what it must be like for ordinary Israelis to try to go about their ordinary every day lives - living with the constant threat of the suicide bomber. I can tell you that Israel's desire for security is not something we in the British Government take for granted. That is why we are pressing the Palestinians to take urgent action against terrorism, to form a government that can take the long overdue steps to improve the security situation in the Occupied Territories.

"A strong stand against terror is essential. This includes not only terror organizations like al-Qaida or the Palestinian rejectionists, but also those who fund, harbour and support them. The recent prescription of Hamas and PIJ by the UK is, I hope, just one example of our determination.

"Supporting the friends of Israel is absolutely fundamental. It is about recognizing the fundamental legitimacy of the State of Israel. There are still those who oppose the very existence of the State of Israel. It is depressing that all of us must constantly restate Israel's right to exist, but we must continue to do so... Britain is, I believe, and as the Prime Minister said many times, Israel's best friend in Europe".

Geoff Hoon, Secretary of State for Defence 13/11/03
(www.parliament.the-stationery-office.com)

"The PA, despite consistent promises by its leadership, has made no progress on its core obligation to take immediate action on the ground to end violence and combat terror, and to reform and reorganize the Palestinian Authority".

Terje Roed-Larsen, UN Middle East Envoy
(The Jerusalem Post, 14/7/04)

"In Israel we see civilians, including children, deliberately targeted by Palestinian suicide bombers".

Kofi Annan, UN Secretary-General,
(www.bicom.org.uk, 21/9/04)

"I will resolutely defend the right of Israel to exist free of terrorism with internationally guaranteed and peaceful borders".

Michael Ancram, Shadow Foreign Secretary,
at Conservative Party Conference, 7/10/04
(www.conservatives.com)

"Any attack on civilians is prohibited by international law, but using children for suicide attacks is particularly egregious. Palestinian armed groups must clearly and publicly condemn all use of children under the age of 18 for military activities, and nothing, but nothing, justifies suicide bombing - the life of every Israeli child is of equal value and precious in the sight of God as that of every Palestinian child".

Menzies Campbell, Shadow Foreign Secretary,
at Liberal Democrat Party Conference, 20/9/04
(www.libdems.org.uk)

"On all issues that bring together demands around the world, Israel actually is a model of democracy in a very difficult region where very little exists.

"And what we need to do, of course, is to have a proper negotiated settlement.   The principles that underpin it [a negotiated settlement] have got to be the absence of terrorism".

Tony Blair, British Prime Minister,
at Labour Friends of Israel fringe meeting, 28/9/04,
(www.totallyjewish.com)

14.

The Middle East "Road Map"
30/5/03

"A two-state solution to the Israeli-Palestine conflict will only be achieved through an end to violence and terrorism, when the Palestinian people have a leadership acting decisively against terror.

"Phase I

All official Palestinian institutions must end incitement against Israel. A reformed Palestinian government must begin sustained, targeted, and effective operations against all terrorist groups operating in its territories.

The Israel leadership must issue an unequivocal statement affirming its commitment to the two-state vision of an independent, viable, sovereign Palestinian state living in peace and security alongside Israel, and call for an immediate end to violence against Palestinians everywhere.

Israel must take all necessary steps to help normalize Palestinian life and must withdraw from areas occupied from September 28, 2000. Israel must also dismantle settlements erected since March 2001 and freeze all other settlement activity".

Christian Science Monitor: (ww.csmonitor.com)
For full text see Appendix L

WORLD VIEW

"Israel withdrew troops from Gaza and Bethlehem and was on the verge of handing over two further towns to Palestinian control, but in the first month of the 'cease fire' there were over 100 attacks against Israelis".

"Christians, Israel, and the Struggle for Peace",
September 2003
(Christian Friends of Israel, www.cfi.org.uk)

15.
"Right of Return"

"For achieving a just settlement of the refugee problem".

UN Security Council Resolution 242, 22/11/67,
(United Nations: www.domino-un.org)
For full text see Appendix G

"Since 1948 we have been demanding the return of the refugees to their homes. But we ourselves are the ones who encouraged them to leave. Only a few months separated our call to them to leave and our appeal to the United Nations to resolve on their return".

Memoirs of Haled al-Am,
Prime Minister of Syria 1948-1949, vol. 1, pp 386-87,
(International Christian Embassy Jerusalem Canada:
www.cdn-friends-icej.ca)

"Every child who was born to a Palestinian Arab father after this date [1948], whether in Palestine or outside, is a Palestinian".

Palestinian National Charter 1964
For full text see Appendix E

"The Palestinian demand for the 'right of return' is totally unrealistic, and would have to be solved by means of financial compensation and resettlement in Arab countries".

President Hosni Mubarak of Egypt, 1989
(www.israelactivism.com)

"The sentence for anyone who accepts compensation for his property is the same sentence meted out in the fatwa issued by religious scholars in the 1930s strictly forbidding (refugees) from accepting compensation (for land). This is because the Palestinian land is not a commodity to be bought and sold; it is a blessed and holy Waqf *[i.e. religious endowment]*

Sheikh Ikrama Sabri, Mufti of Jerusalem and the Palestinian Lands, in a fatwa on 1/12/03, to the National Conference for the Defense of the Right of Return, at the Rashad Shawa Center in Gaza. Al-Hayat Al-Jadida (PA), 2/12/03, (Middle East Media Research Institute: www.memri.org)

Resettle the Palestinian refugees in a Palestinian state "not in a way that would undermine the existence of Israel as a predominantly Jewish state. Otherwise what does a two-state solution mean?".

Sari Nusseibeh, top PLO representative in Jerusalem, in AP interview, September 2000 (Associated Press: www.ap.org)

"To us, the refugees issue is the winning card which means the end of the Israeli state".

Sakher Habash, member of Fatah Central Committee, at a seminar on "The Palestinian Refugee from the Political Parties' Perspective", Al-Najah University, 23/11/04, (www.fateh.org_public/refugees.htm, 12/9/04)

WORLD VIEWS

"'Return' clearly cannot apply to the movement of any person to a country to which he has never previously been".

F.O telegram to Washington 4/12/1948. Ref: 12149, FO 371/51126/WR3268

"There is no doubt in my mind that those *[Jewish]* refugees from Egypt who are not able or not willing to avail themselves of the protection of the Government of their nationality fall under the mandate of my office".

Auguste Lindt, High Commissioner, at meeting of United Nations Refugee Executive Committee, Geneva, 29/1/57, ("Justice for Jews from Arab Countries", 17/10/03: www.jewishrefugees.org)

"Jews from Middle Eastern and North African countries who have left or are unable or unwilling to return to these countries in consequence of recent events fall within the mandate of the commission".

Dr E. Jahn, UN High Commission for Refugees, July 1967 ("Myths and Facts 1976", Near East Report, Washington, 1976)

16.
Jerusalem

"The claims of historic and spiritual ties between Jews and Palestine are not in agreement with the facts of history".

Palestinian National Charter (www.palestine-un.org)
For full text see Appendix D

"Second Temple referenced in the Bible... Not only is there overwhelming - even undisputable - archaeological proof of the temple's presence in Jerusalem, Muslim authorities in Jerusalem once acknowledged it themselves".

Joseph Farah, Arab-American journalist, 14/9/03
(www.worldnetdaily.com)

"I would be blind to disclaim the Jewish connection to Jerusalem...The existential connection Jews have to Jerusalem needs to be recognised and respected, just as the Islamic and Arab connection to Jerusalem must be".

Sari Nusseibeh, President of Al Quds University,
East Jerusalem, November 2000
(www.internationalwallofprayer.org)

"The Koran says nothing about Jerusalem. It mentions Mecca hundreds of times. It mentions Medina countless times. It never mentions Jerusalem. With good reason. There is no historical evidence to suggest Mohammed ever visited Jerusalem".

Joseph Farah, Arab-American journalist, 8/1/02
(www.worldnetdaily.com)

"The mosque known today as the Al-Aqsa Mosque is not the one referred to by the Koranic words: 'From the Al-Harem Mosque [in Mecca] to the most distant mosque [Al-Aqsa]'..... Jerusalem was no longer the centre of worship for the followers of Muhammed.   Aelia [Jerusalem] was the centre of worship for the Jews, as it continues to be".

Ahmad Muhammad 'Arafa,
columnist for Egyptian weekly Al-Qahira,
published by Egyptian Ministry of Culture, 5/9/03
(Middle East Media Research Institute, www.memri.org)

WORLD VIEW

"The first authoritative census of the city [Jerusalem] in 1844, discovered that 7,120 of Jerusalem's 12,510 inhabitants were Jewish - and this before there was a west or new Jerusalem. Thus even the Old City of Jerusalem had a Jewish majority well over a century ago".

http://www.thomas.loc.gov
[There has been a continuous Jewish presence in Jerusalem from biblical times, and a Jewish majority since 1844]

17.

Israel's Temporary
Security Fence 2003

Israel Information Center (www.mfa.gov.il)

Section of Temporary
Security Fence

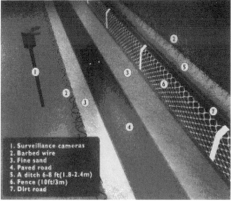

1. Surveillance cameras
2. Barbed wire
3. Fine sand
4. Paved road
5. A ditch 6-8 ft(1.8-2.4m)
6. Fence (10ft/3m)
7. Dirt road

Israel Information Center (www.mfa.gov.il)

...permit an occupying power "to take action including the erection of a fence, if it deems this necessary for security needs".

1907 Hague Regulations and 4th Geneva Convention

"Israel shall continue to carry the responsibility ...for overall security of Israelis and settlements, for the purpose of safeguarding their internal security and public order, and will have all the powers to take the steps necessary to meet this responsibility".

Israeli-Palestinian Interim Agreement on the West Bank and Gaza strip, Washington D.C., 18/9/95, Article XII Para I

"Nothing in the article shall derogate from Israel's security powers and responsibilities in accordance with this agreement".

Israeli-Palestinian Interim Agreement on the West Bank and Gaza strip, Washington D.C., 18/9/95, Annex I, Article I Redeployment of Israeli Military Forces and Transfer of Responsibility, Para 7

"Nothing in the present Charter shall impair the inherent right of individual or collective self-defense if an armed attack occurs against a Member of the United Nations, until the United Nations has taken measures necessary to maintain inter-national peace and security".

Article 51 of the Charter of the United Nations

"Article 51 of the Charter [of the United Nations] thus recognizes the existence of an inherent right of self-defence in the case of armed attack by one State against another State. However, Israel does not claim that the attacks against it are imputable to a foreign State".

Clause 139, International Criminal Court of Justice, The Hague, 10/7/04

"Israel is under an obligation to terminate its breaches of international law; it is under an obligation to cease forthwith the works of construction of the wall being built in the Occupied Palestinian Territory, including in and around East Jerusalem, to dismantle forthwith the structure therein situated".

International Criminal Court of Justice, The Hague, 10/7/04

"Had they *[the Palestinians]* agreed to...accept the principles of the Camp David Agreement, they would not have made it possible for Israel to establish the settlements and the separation fence, and would not have needed to make all these concessions".

Said Sunbal, Al-Akhbar (Egypt) 24/12/03
(Middle East Media Research Institute: www.memri.org)

"When we hear of spontaneous marches in the streets of the Arab and Muslim countries condemning the suicide and terror operations aimed at innocent people in Israel and other places, and demands for trials for those who encourage them - then the fence will fall without using a single axe".

Bassam Darwish, editor of www.annaqed.com,
"A Complex Waiting to be Solved", 16/10/03
(Middle East Media Research Institute: www.memr.org)

"The Palestine Leadership stresses that its foremost national interest demands that such acts [suicide bombings] stop as they serve as excuses for Israel to continue building its wall".

Arafat's website, 22/2/04
(Independent Media Review Analysis: www.imra.org.il)

"No fence can cut me off from my people, but I also want security, I also want peace. Since the government put up the fence, you haven't had one case of an attacker that came through Umm al-Fahm."

"Residents are sleeping peacefully, they feel more secure. People aren't passing through their houses and their fields, they are not blowing up anything and not endangering the residents".

Sheikh Hashem Abd a-Rahman, Mayor of Umm al-Fahm,
(Haaretz, 11/7/04)

"The Palestinians and their suicide attacks are what forced Israel to build a fence".

Tawfik Abu Baker, Palestinian parliamentary member,
Al Dastour, Jordan, 7/1/04,
("The Anti-Terror Fence", Israel, MFA 2004)

"Yasser Arafat, the PA and the militant fundamentalists are responsible for building this fence. No one else built it".

Dr Ahsan Al Trabelsi, publicist,,"Ilaf" website, 13/1/04,
("The Anti-Terror Fence", Israel, MFA 2004)

"Had the Arabs accepted an agreement with Israel three years ago, they would have saved 1500 Palestinian lives, and prevented the building of the fence".

Abed El Rahman Rashid, editorial,
"Al Sharq Al Awsat", 12/12/03,
("The Anti-Terror Fence", Israel, MFA 2004)

WORLD VIEWS

"Since the fence built around the Gaza Strip has been in place, almost all the suicide bombings have come from the West Bank - indeed, I believe that only one has come from the Gaza Strip. I am sure that that unites Israeli public opinion around the feeling that there is a real necessity for the fence, for the sake of their own security. On 14th October the Security Council voted on a text that demanded Israel should cease the construction of the fence. We considered that that draft had insufficient references to terrorism and, therefore, that it was unbalanced and unhelpful to the implementation of the road map".

Baroness Symons of Vernham Dean 28/10/03
(www.publications.parliament.uk/cgi-bin/dialogserver TSO)

"The security fence....is, for the most part, a rather fragile barbed-wire fence, with electronic sensors to detect the passage of any would-be suicide bombers. A similar fence surrounds the Gaza strip, where it has successfully ensured that not one local suicide bomber has ever penetrated Israel proper".

George Keravan, The Scotsman, 12/1/04

"I fail to understand the Court's view that an occupying power loses the right to defend its own civilian citizens at home if the attacks emanate from the occupied territory - Palestine cannot be sufficiently an international entity to be invited to these proceedings, and to benefit from humanitarian law, but not sufficiently an international entity for the prohibition of armed attack on others to be applicable".

(British) Judge Rosalyn Higgins,
The Jerusalem Post, 26/7/04

"The protection of civilians remains an intransgressible obligation of humanitarian law, not only for the occupier but equally for those seeking to liberate themselves from occupation".

David Pannick, The Times, 27/7/04

"Those who draw comparisons with the Berlin Wall are wrong, because it does not shut people in and deprive them of their freedom. Its purpose is to protect Israel from terrorists".

Otto Schily, German Interior Minister, 14/9/04
(www.dw-world.de)

"We are not interested to continue dealing with the issue of the separation fence within the parameters of the United Nations. The opinion on the fence given by the International Court of Justice in The Hague is advisory and does not require that deliberations on the issue continue in the General Assembly."

EU Diplomat, (Haaretz, 15/9/04)

"I have always defended Israel's right to defend itself. I go further, I think it is one of the first duties of a Government to protect its citizens...I support the building of the security wall in so far as it is there to defend citizens of Israel from suicide attacks".

Michael Ancram, Shadow Foreign Secretary,
at Conservative Party Conference, 5/10/04
(www.conservatives.com)

18.

Geneva Accords 2003

"Our aim was to create divisions inside Israel and block the growth of the right-wing in Israel. We didn't get the OK from Arafat, and this paved the way for street protests. We can't go to Geneva without Arafat's consent".

Hatem Abdel Kader, Fatah negotiator,
in interview with Khaled Abu Toameh,
The Jerusalem Post, 30/11/03 (www.wnd.com)

19.

Disengagement 2003

"It is not in our interest to govern you. We would like you to govern yourselves in your own country. A democratic Palestinian state with territorial contiguity in Judea and Samaria and economic viability, which would conduct normal relations of tranquility, security, and peace with Israel".

"However, if in a few months the Palestinians still continue to disregard their part in implementing the Roadmap, then Israel will initiate the unilateral security step of disengagement from the Palestinians. The Disengagement Plan is a security measure and not a political one. The steps which will be taken will not prevent the possibility of returning to the implementation of the Roadmap and reaching an agreed settlement".

Ariel Sharon, Herzliya Conference, December 2000
(Jerusalem Center for Public Affairs: www.jcpa.org)

"Sharon is trying again to escape the roadmap plan backed by the United States and the international community".

Ghassan Khatib, 22/12/03
on Sharon's disengagement plan
(www.bitterlemons-international.org)

"Prime Minister Sharon is a pragmatic man who wants security for his people, but is unable to find a partner on the Palestinian side with whom to conduct negotiations".

Prince Hassan bin Talal, uncle of Jordan's King
Abdullah, in Italian newspaper "La Stampa", January 2004,
(Jerusalem Report 29/01/04: www.jrep.com, 12/1/04)

"With no more Israeli patrols taking place, as they do now, the security situation will deteriorate on Israel's fence. The terrorists will develop new tactics and buy new weapons including weapons of mass destruction".

Joseph Farah, Arab-American journalist, January 2002
(www.worldnetdaily.com)

"It was the Israeli left and your peace-camp that ultimately encouraged us to continue with our suicide attacks....The disengagement from Gaza is proof of our victory. The fact is that Sharon is willing to withdraw unconditionally, and is essentially raising a white flag and retreating. Only by force can we teach the other side what to do".

A Hamas leader, as quoted by Yisacharov
on Israel's Channel 1 Television, 9/9/04
(www.fliegler.org)

WORLD VIEWS

"Recalling all its previous relevant resolutions, in particular resolutions 242 (1967) and 338 (1973), affirming a vision of a region where two States, Israel and Palestine, live side by side within secure and recognized borders".

Security Council Resolution 1397, 12/3/02
(www.un.org)
For full text see Appendix K

"Peace for Israel means security, and we must stand with all our might to protect its right to exist, its territorial integrity. I see Israel as one of the great outposts of democracy in the world, and a marvelous example of what can be done, how desert land can be transformed into an oasis of brotherhood and democracy. Peace for Israel means security and that security must be a reality".

Martin Luther King, in a speech on 25/3/68,
(www.jewish-history.com/mlk_zionism.html)

"An Israeli withdrawal from the Gaza Strip has the earmarks of such a (bold) step. We anxiously await the details and timetable for the withdrawal and urge the Palestinians to meet the plan with meaningful reciprocal confidence-building measures - most imperatively in the area of security".

Terje Roed-Larsen, UN Middle East envoy
(17/2/04, Associated Press: www.ap.org)

"You are aware... that the Palestinian side too has obligations it has not fulfilled. The Palestinian Authority should immediately start taking effective measures to curb terrorism and violence... Decisive actions would help the international community ensure that any withdrawal from Gaza is part of the implementation of the road map and not a substitute for it."

Kofi Annan, UN Secretary-General, 29/4/04, (Reuters)

"Fate, in the shape of Sharon, is giving Arafat a last chance to show he is a leader, rather than an obstacle to peace".

Anton La Guardia,
The Daily Telegraph, 21/10/04

20.

Arafat

"You understand that we plan to eliminate the State of Israel and establish a purely Palestinian state...I have no use for Jews; they are, and remain Jews".

Arafat, Grand Hotel, Stockholm, 30/1/96
(www.accessmiddleeast.org)

"Mr Arafat should quit his position because he is the head of a corrupt authority. There is no point for him to remain in politics...He has destroyed Palestine. He has led it to terrorism, death and a hopeless situation. He has also divided the country...All Arab leaders know this fact. It won't be possible for us to gain from the Middle East road map for peace if this man remains in power".

Ahmed Al-Jarallah, Arab Times, Kuwait
(The Guardian, 19/7/04)

"Tens of thousands of Palestinians have been killed in Lebanon and Jordan and now in Palestine because of your systematic corruption ever since you came to power in 1968...You must release the people from your grip and corrupt authority. The solution is that you pack your bags and leave together with all the corrupt officials. Go anywhere you choose - Egypt, Tunis, or Tel Aviv, anywhere. Just go, go, go".

Dr. Ibrahim Hammami, London-based
Palestinian writer in open letter to Arafat
(The Jerusalem Post, 27/7/04)

"Arafat and top PA officials did not respect the rule of law; many were corrupt.

"By 1996 Palestinians in the PA were saying that they had traded one occupation for two, the one by Israel, and one by Arafat and his cronies. Rather than use donor funds for their intended purposes, Arafat regularly diverted money to his own accounts.

"Arafat's failed leadership is one factor responsible for the evolution of Palestinian extremism and fundamentalism, as well as a culture of death and despair among Palestinians".

Issam Abu Issa, former chairman of the
Palestine International Bank, and founder of the Palestinian
National Coalition for Democracy and Independence,
Middle East Quarterly, Fall 2004: www.meforum.org/article 645

WORLD VIEWS

"Arafat has ruled in a dictatorial manner, employing many separate police forces, and carrying out torture of detainees, arbitrary arrest, prolonged arbitrary detention...executions after grossly unfair trials, [and failing] to bring justice to those responsible for vigilante killings".

Human Rights Watch, 26/1/01
(www.hrw/reports 2001)

"He is a career terrorist, trained, armed and bankrolled by the Soviet Union and its satellites for decades...The KGB remoulded Arafat as a rabid anti-Zionist. They also selected a 'personal hero' for him - the Grand Mufti Haj Aminal-Husseini, the man who visited Auschwitz in the late 1930s and reproached the Germans for not having killed even more Jews.

" 'You simply have to keep on pretending that you'll break with terrorism and that you'll recognise Israel - over, and over, and over' Ceaucescu told him".

Ion Mihai Pacepa, highest ranking intelligence
officer ever to have defected from the Soviet bloc,
Wall Street Journal, 22/9/03

"But if you really want to know why the Palestinian people live in such appalling squalor, then look no further than this week's revelation that Yasser Arafat has managed to squirrel away a staggering £1.8 billion. His wife gets £60,000 a month just for spending money".

Mitchell Symon, The Daily Express, 14/11/03

"All attempts to end the fighting have foundered on the conundrum that is Arafat....But if he cannot or will not make the guns fall silent, what is the point of seeking a deal with him?....Arafat refuses to go away. But, a growing number of Palestinians, even close lieutenants of the 'president', believe he is leading them to disaster".

Anton La Guardia, The Daily Telegraph, 21/10/04

"One of the reasons his credibility as a leader was undermined on the Palestinian side was an increasing agreement among the leadership and the Palestinian people that Arafat had led them in the wrong direction over the past four years."

Terje Roed-Larsen,
UN Middle East envoy, Haaretz, 11/11/04

21.

The Palestinian Authority

"Article 2. Palestine, with its boundaries at the time of the British Mandate, is an indivisible territorial unit.

Article 4. The people of Palestine determine its destiny when it completes the liberation of its homeland. *[At this time, Israel's borders were the cease-fire line of 1948]*

Article 17. The partitioning of Palestine, which took place in 1947, and the establishment of Israel are illegal and null and void.

Article 18. The Balfour Declaration, the Palestine Mandate system, and all that has been based on them are considered null and void".

Palestinian National Charter 1964
(www.palestine-un.org)
For full text see Appendix D

Article 15. The liberation of Palestine ...aims at the elimination of Zionism in Palestine

Article 22. ...the liberation of Palestine will destroy the Zionist and imperialist presence".

The PLO Charter, 1968
For full text see Appendix H
(www.netaxss.com)

Preamble. "Israel will exist and will continue to exist until Islam will obliterate it, just as it obliterated others before it".

Article 13. "[Peace] initiatives, and so-called peaceful solutions and international conferences are in contradiction to the principles of the Islamic Resistance Movement....There is no solution for the Palestinian problem except by Jihad".

Article 32. Zionism scheming has no end....Their scheme has been laid out in the 'Protocols of Zion'".

The Covenant of Hamas, August 1988
(www.fas.org)

"There are no differences between Jordanians, Palestinians, Syrians and Lebanese. We are all part of one nation. It is only for political identity.... Yes, the existence of a separate Palestinian identity serves only tactical purposes. The founding of a Palestinian state is a new tool in the continuing battle against Israel".

Zuheir Muhsin, late Military Department head of the PLO and member of its Executive Council, Dutch daily Trouw, March 1977

"There is no language known as Palestinian. There is no distinct Palestinian culture. There has never been a land known as Palestine governed by Palestinians".

Joseph Farah, Arab-American journalist, January 2002
(www.worldnetdaily.com)

"If they go from Sheba'a, we will not stop fighting them. Our goal is to liberate the 1948 borders of Palestine...[Jews] can go back to Germany or wherever they came from".

Hassan Ezzedin, Hizbollah spokesperson,
New Yorker, 14/10/02
(www.jewishvirtualibrary,org)

"We took gigantic risks to be here because... we want Israelis to know that there are lots of Palestinians who support peace and who you never see in the media".

25-year-old Majid Belay, from the
Youth Federation of Nablus, a West Bank city
best known as a center of terrorism, 28/2/03
(Middle East Media Research Institute: www.memri.org)

"It is time for the world and civilized nations not to consider the Palestinian Authority as representative of a people, of having a place among the nations, but rather as a gang promoting terror, educating children in terror from elementary school age.   The tragedy is that this organization receives funds and donations".

Sheikh Palazzi, Secretary General of
Italian Muslim Association, 12/3/03
(www.mideasttruth.com)

"The Palestinian intellectuals do not really care about the suffering of their people. Most of them live in fancy houses in the U.S. or Europe, [drive] luxury cars, and [send] their children to attend prestigious schools. And every time a solution to the Palestinian problem is proposed they say 'No' [and choose] steadfastness, sacrifice, and Shahada [martyrdom]. And who is the shahid [martyr]? Not any of their sons. Not at all. Rather, one of the children of the unfortunate [Palestinians]".

Khaled Al-Qishtine, An Iraqi Intellectual in London:
"Arab Nationalists' Interference in Iraqi Affairs
Will Pound the Final Nail Into Iraq's Coffin",
"Elaph" website, 31/7/03
(Middle East Media Research Institute:www.memri.org)

"What is the Al-Aqsa Martyr's Brigade? It is not a cell of al-Qaida. It is not a cell of Hamas. It is not a cell of Hezbollah. It is, however, a cell of Fatah, the same organization founded and directed by Arafat and Mazen for nearly 40 years".

Joseph Farah, Arab-American journalist, July 2003
(www.worldnetdaily.com)

"The religious discourse brainwashing people day and night on the government [and] public satellite [television] channels is a blatant expression of the backward mentality that does not believe in the other and refuses to coexist with him".

Abu Ahmad Mustafa, reformist Arab diplomat, in
London Arabic-language daily "Al-Sharq Al-Awsat", 13/9/03
(Middle East Media Research Institute: www.memri.org)

"As the Palestinian women mourn their sons, their brothers, and their fathers, the sheikhs and the leaders [scuffling]   for chairs and salaries arise. This leadership wants neither a solution nor land; nothing interests it except its own personal battles".   ˙

Editor of London's Al-Sharq Al-Awsat Daily:
"Arafat and Abu Mazen Must Go" 29/8/2003,
(Middle East Media Research Institute: www.memri.org)

"Our leadership ... enabled [the Zionists] to succeed at every opportunity through political means, with its 'all or nothing' policy, by rejecting every proposal for compromise".

Tawfiq Abu Bakr, Liberal Palestinian writer,
Al-Ayyam, PA daily, September 14, 2003
(Middle East Media Research Institute: www.memri.org)

"Are these scum of the earth capable of accomplishing something for the Palestinian people? It is reasonable to assume that they, like the supporters of suicide bombings, are the first to damage the Palestinian cause, and are bringing death upon the Palestinian people".

Hazem Abd Al-Rahman, Al-Ahram (Egypt), 24/12/03,
(Middle East Media Research Institute:www.memri.org)

"The rabble majority of the Arab and Palestinian street today refuse to accept any kind of a peace agreement with Israel...It is they who applaud the bus and restaurant bombings in order to destroy any spark of hope for peace".

Sami Buheiri, Egyptian columnist, Al-Ahram
30/12/03 (www.elaph.com)

"In my opinion, the area of Palestine is already divided into a Jewish Palestinian State (Israel) and an Arab Palestinian State (Jordan). Creating a third Palestinian state for the PLO is neither in the interest of Israel, nor in the interest of Jordan, and even less in the interests of those Arabs who would be compelled to live under that kind of barbaric regime. Moreover, accepting the creation of such a state would mean that terror works, and must be rewarded; it would represent a defeat of legality and an undue encouragement to terrorist groups".

Sheikh Palazzi, Secretary General of Italian Muslim
Association interview with Israpundit, 4/12/03,
(www.israpundit.com)

"The worst enemy of the Palestinian cause is the Palestinians, who have endorsed a policy of refusal and fundamentalist extremism as a way of behaviour".

Jubran Tuwe, Lebanese daily Al-Nahar, January 2004,
(Middle East Media Research Institute: www.memri.org)

"Israel, the State of Israel, is the Satan's offspring....cannot exist among human beings".

Ahmad Nasser, Secretary of Palestinian
Legislative Council, on PATV 6/2/04
(Palestine Media Watch: www.pmw.org.il)

"Most Jews believe in a two-state solution. I do not believe in this. A Palestinian state will concoct its own rules and laws to continue the killing of Jews....Never in history was there a Palestinian state. We never wanted a Palestinian state - even today the Palestinians do not want a Palestinian state. They want the destruction of the Jews. It's a religious holy war. It's in the culture, the tradition".

Walid Shoebat, former PLO terrorist,
Israel National News, 27/1/04
(www.factsofisrael.com)

"Corruption has reached non-governmental institutions and many other bodies and organizations...The people are asking what happened to the huge sums of money earmarked for the Palestinians' welfare."

Samir Masharawi, PLC Member,
The Jerusalem Post, 4/10/04,
(www.bicom.org.uk)

"There's no one to punish these corrupt officials...That's why corruption cases are being dealt with in a careless manner."

Rawya Shawwa, PLC Member,
The Jerusalem Post, 4/10/04
(www.bicom.org.uk)

"Two years ago, a few proud Beduin Israeli citizens like myself asked: what is our position and status in the State of Israel in the midst of its current situation? After all, Beduins are part of Israel's success story. During current times, when Israel is being attacked and accused of being a racist state, an 'aggressor and an oppressor', we decided that the smallest and probably most effective thing we could do is to spread our story as part of Israeli society".

Ismail Khaldi, an Israeli Beduin, graduated from Tel Aviv university with an MA in political science, served with Israel Police, IDF, and the Defence Ministry, and worked at the U.S Embassy in Tel Aviv, 3/11/04 (www.israel21c.org/bin/en.jsp)

WORLD VIEWS

"Their goal, apart from the overthrow of Israel, is not some cosy utopia where you can drink champagne at a new gallery opening. They are against any two-state solution in Palestine, period. Cutting off US aid to Israel or demolishing the West Bank settlements would do nothing to curb their murderous intent. Giving them any intellectual comfort is naïve at best, and criminal at worst".

George Keravan
The Scotsman, 6/10/03

"The financial support which is given to the Palestinian Authority [by the EU], should not be used for anti-Jewish propaganda".

Dirk Niebel MP, Hildegard Muller MP,
in letter to German Foreign Minister, November 2004
(www.pmw.org.il)

Palestinian Authority instruction of Children

"Martyred Jihad fighters are the most honoured people, after the prophets".

Reader for Literary Texts for 8th, 9th,
and 10th grades in Palestine Authority
("Incitement, Hatred and Trends from the Palestinian Press
and Textbooks", Israel Information Centre, 2003)

"The honourable soul has two objectives: achieving death and honour".

Song of the Martyr, 6th grade, Palestine Authority,
("Incitement, Hatred and Trends from the Palestinian
Press and Textbooks", Israel Information Center 2003)

"In the lesson of the day, the Sheikh sat smiling and said: 'Oh children, write the Hadith [you learned] today. It is the message to continue the Jihad until the day the dead are resurrected and the Muslims, the Jihad fighters, are victorious against the Jews and their followers, the enemies of Allah. We are [in the month] Ramadan, which is the month of Jihad".

A Ramadan story entitled "The Jihad-Fighting Group",
16th issue of Al-Fateh, an on-line children's
newspaper published by Hamas
(www.memri.org)

"And the Jew will hide behind the stone and the tree, and the stone and the tree will say: 'O servant of Allah, Oh Muslim, this is a Jew behind me. Come and Kill him!' The resurrection will not come before this happens".

> *Sheikh Yusef Al Qaradawi, quoting from the Quran,*
> *Hadith of Ibn-Omar and the Hadith of Abu-Hurairah,*
> *in a speech to the Muslim Arab Youth*
>
> *Association conference in Ohio, USA, in 1995*
> *(www.goodislam.com)*

WORLD VIEWS - on Palestinian Authority Education

"The child shall be protected from practices which may foster racial, religious and any other form of discrimination. He shall be brought up in a spirit of understanding, tolerance, friendship among peoples, peace and universal brotherhood, and in full consciousness that his energy and talents should be devoted to the service of his fellow men".

> *U.N Office of the High Commissioner for Human*
> *Rights, Declaration of the Rights of the Child,*
> *Principle 10, proclaimed by General Assembly*
> *resolution 1386 (XIV), 20/1/59*
> *(www.un.org)*

"The child who has been taught to die and to kill from kindergarten on, via song and slogan in praise of bloodletting, represents an inconceivable cultural ideal".

> *Cynthia Ozick, "Quarrel and Quandary: Essays"*
> *(Knopf, 2000)*

"Because of the authority's incapacity to lead, suicide bombing and foolish diplomacy are defining the Palestinian national agenda, without the consent of the Palestinian people. Killing innocent Israeli civilians alienates Israeli and Western public opinion and undermines the indispensable moral and ethical legitimacy of the Palestinian cause".

David Pryce-Jones,
The Spectator, 14/11/03

"I find also any language that validates, justifies the use of scrambling the brains of young boys and girls to go and blow up innocent women and children in buses is also unacceptable".

Denis MacShane, UK Minister for Europe,
The Guardian, 3/3/04

"The ongoing and cynical use of children by Palestinian groups in armed conflict is a flagrant breach of international law and it must stop.

Children of the Middle East are the future. The key to a true and lasting peace in the region is in the education of the next generation in the values of co-existence and understanding. The international community's ongoing silence on this issue continues to leave both Palestinian and Israeli children defenseless".

Lord Clark of Hampstead, Lord Janner of Braunstone,
Lord Jacobs, Lord Hogg of Cumbernauld,
Baroness Miller of Hampstead,
The Independent, 29/6/04

"It must be stated that, in very real terms, a Palestinian state already exists in the present state of Jordan. In 1946, when Britain determined to establish Eastern Palestine as an independent sovereign Arab state, King Abdullah wanted to call the area Palestine. He was dissuaded from this by the British, and instead the new independent state was called TransJordan and later renamed Jordan. The fact is that today Jordan's population is 52 -77% Palestinian whose people can, and do, travel to and from the 'West Bank'".

"Where is the Land of Palestine",
Christian Friends of Israel, 2003,
(www.cfi.org.uk)

Palestinian Authority on Christians

"Allah the almighty has called upon us not to ally with the Jews or Christians, not to like them, not to become their partners, not to support them, and not to sign agreements with them".

Dr. Ahmad Abu Halabiya, in a sermon from a Gaza
mosque, broadcast on official PA TV, 13/10/2000
(www.memri.org.il)

"They hate us Christians more than they love Palestine".

Sayed Anwar, Washington Times, 13/5/02

"The idea was to enter the church [of the Nativity, Bethlehem] in order to create international pressure on Israel. We knew beforehand that there was two years' worth of food for fifty monks".

Abdullah Abu-Hadid, senior Tanzim commander, 30/5/02
(Jerusalem Center for Public Affairs: jcpa.org)

WORLD VIEWS

"Life in (PA ruled) Bethlehem has become insufferable for many members of the dwindling Christian minorities. Increasing Muslim-Christian tensions have left some Christians reluctant to celebrate Christmas in the town at the heart of the story of Christ's birth".

Report in The Times, London, December 1997
(www.copts.net)

Palestinian Authority's instructions to Journalists

"The Palestinian journalists union declared...that news photographers are forbidden from taking pictures of Palestinian children carrying weapons or taking part in activities by 'militant groups' saying that the pictures harm the Palestinian cause".

Yahoo 27/8/03
(www.dailynews.yahoo.com)

"Being balanced, according to their [journalists'] mandate, can be frustrating, so present your stories on a human level and do not rely on the facts".

Palestinian Academic Society for the
Study of International Affairs, November 2003
(www.coldfury.com)

22.

The Arab World and Iran

"Facts About the Middle East", othersideofthecoin, 2004,
(www.otherside.sphosting.com)

"Come out openly, like Iran, and say you don't accept such a country as Israel on the world map. Have courage. We can make good use of our weapons, military equipment and all our forces".

Ali Akbar, speaker of the Iranian parliament,
speaking to Arab nations, 1999
(Independent Media Review Analysis: www.imra.org.il)

"The cancerous tumour called Israel must be uprooted from the region".

Ali Khamenei, Supreme Leader of Iran, 15/12/2000 ,
(Independent Media Review Analysis: www.imra.org.il)

"Muhammad ibn Abd Al-Wahhab [who maintained that] 'Islam is the one true religion... and the other religions are false' [claimed that] Islam is even the absolute future of Djinns: 'It is essential that the entire world, men and Djinns alike, enter the framework of Islam...and if not, their fate will be hell".

Tunisian Intellectual Al-Afif Al-Akhdar on the Arab Identity
Crisis and Education in the Arab World, September 2003,
(Middle East Media Research Institute: www.memri.org)

"The woman must be taught how to fight within the home, how to put together an explosive belt and blow herself up...Women must be taught to booby trap their clothes closets, booby-trap their purses, booby-trap their shoes, booby-trap the children's toys, so they blow up on the enemy soldiers".

Col. Mu'ammar Al-Qaddafi,
to a group of women in city of Sabha, 4/10/03
(Middle East Media Research Institute, www.memri.org)

"If one day the Muslim world will be equipped with the weapons that Israel has now, that will bring the world's arrogance to a dead end, since the use of one nuclear bomb against Israel will leave nothing on the face of the earth, whereas to the Islamic world it will only inflict damage".

Hashemi-Rafsanjani, Iranian leader,
in an Al-Quds day sermon, 2001
(www.worldtribune.com)

"The foundation of the Islamic regime is opposition to Israel, and the perpetual subject of Iran is the elimination of Israel from the region".

Ayatollah Ali Khameni, January 2001,
(www.honestreporting.com)

"Israel will not be a legitimate state even if peace is accomplished".

Bashar Al-Assad, Syrian President, interview
with Syrian daily Al-Safiri (Lebanon), 31/3/03,
(Middle East Media Research Institute: www.memri.org)

"Why do expressions of tolerance, moderation, rationalism, compromise, and negotiation horrify us, but [when we hear] fervent cries for vengeance, we all dance the war dance?"

Tunisian Intellectual Al-Afif Al-Akhdar on the Arab Identity
Crisis and Education in the Arab World, September 2003,
(Middle East Media Research Institute:www.memri.org)

"Everything that happened to the Palestinians as a result of their being dragged after the leaders of words, who for over half a century waved the motto of complete liberation from the [Jordan] river to the [Mediterranean] sea, until we lost nearly everything and Palestine was left practically without a river and without a sea, was not enough for them".

Mursey Atallah, editor, Al-Ahram (Egypt), 23/12/03,
(Middle East Media Research Institute: www.memri.org)

"These regimes are not based on democracy and their legitimacy comes from military dictatorships or inherited systems. The basic right of an individual to voice his or her opinion is not granted in any kind of form in the Arab world".

Ibrahim Nawar, Egyptian human rights champion,
The Daily Telegraph, 13/1/04

"Those who talk about American occupation in Iraq are themselves occupying their countries. They are the colonialists of their peoples, using secret services, agents, whips, jails, and torture dungeons whose walls are smeared with the blood of innocent victims. [When we hear these people] we should remember that no one is a better authority on modesty than a prostitute".

'The New Iraq Will Be the Beacon of Freedom, Democracy,
and Respect to Human Rights in the Middle East',
Editor of the Kuwaiti Daily Al-Siyassa: 10/11/02,
(Middle East Media Research Institute: www.memri.org)

"The answer does not lie in Islam; it is hidden in sick minds brainwashed with hatred for the brethren living nearby and people living thousands of miles away".

Abu Ahmad Mustafa, Arab diplomat, in London
Arabic-language daily Al-Sharq Al-Awsat, 13/9/03,
(Middle East Media Research Institute: www.memri.org)

"There is a dominance of undemocratic practices in the governing regimes of the Arab countries. Elections are mismanaged; women's participation is significantly limited; civil society organisations continue to face considerable constraints in effectively playing an active role; major control over civic association by the authorities is widespread; and media is largely affected by the undemocratic authorities' proliferation in the region".

Zlad Abdel Samad, Executive Director of the Arab
NGO Network Development (ANND),
interview with Bitterlemons, 8/1/04
(www.bitterlemons-international.org)

"The Arab nations keep the Palestinians and their descendants in squalor. They are denied citizenship rights. They are denied work. They are denied property. They are denied their human rights because they are and always will be a political football in the Arab campaign against Israel".

Joseph Farah, Arab-American journalist, 23/4/02
(www.worldnetdaily.com)

"The first thing we learned growing up [in Jericho] was to hate Jews".

Walid Shoebat, former PLO terrorist,
University of Toronto, 27/1/04
(www.israelforum.com)

"Israelis might have nuclear bombs but we have the children bomb and these human bombs must continue until liberation".

Yusuf al-Qaradawi, Islamic Cleric
(The Sun, 6/7/04)

"There is in Israel an amount of democracy that cannot be found in any Arab state".

Jihad al Hazen, senior commentator and columnist,
London-based Al Hayat, 10/8/04
(www.kokhavipublications.com)

"We have become the most terrorist nation and the greatest spillers of blood in the world....What caused the Arabs to lose the rationality with which they led the world in the 10th century? Why have the Arabs gone crazy in such a manner?....Did this...occur because of the rule of the dark religious educational system which incites to war against modernity, democracy, and the new liberalism, and permits the spilling of blood of its supporters, pioneers, and students?....The Arabs think in a medieval fashion regarding politics, society, the economy, and education, even if [they do this] by way of modern electronics".

Dr. Shaker Al-Nabulsi, www.rezgar.com, 14/8/04
(www.memri.org)

"I was raised in Lebanon where I was taught that the Jews were evil, Israel was the devil and the only time we will have peace in the Middle East is when we kill all the Jews and drive them into the sea....It is obvious that Arab terrorism is caused not by the 'desperation' of 'occupation', but by the VERY THOUGHT of a Jewish state. It's time to all stand up and support and defend the state of Israel, which is front line of the war against terrorism".

Brigitte Gabriel, a Lebanese citizen,
in a speech at Duke's University, USA, 14/10/04
(www.yzoa.org)

"I was told not to take any candy from strangers since it could be a Jew trying to poison me. We were told Jews were devils and evil and the enemies of God. It took me many years to realize that Israel is not a threat to the Arab world and is actually an asset in the area".

Nonie Darwish, an Arab who grew up in the Middle
East, in interview with The Jerusalem Post, 27/12/04

"Most of the Arab leaders have used the Palestinian cause in order to divert attention from their abuse of human [rights]....We aren't threatened by America and Israel....We are threatened by terrorist groups, because we move forward".

Ali Salem, Egyptian playwright,
in an interview on Egyptian TV, 18/10/04
(www.memritv.org/Transcript, Clip No. 296)

"Amir Taheri estimates that the Islamist propaganda machine's bill to be about 100 billion dollars during the last two decades alone, which makes it the largest propaganda machine in history, even larger than the communist propaganda machine during the Soviet era. People wouldn't obviously spend that much unless they know they have to defend a huge lie....Since the early 1990's a turn for the worst was inaugurated by the advent of satellite TV. In the Arab world, this important tool of communication is so far completely monopolized by fundamentalism....Freedom in the West gave Islamist terror masters ample opportunity to mount an effective propaganda machine....Only Arab/Muslim secular forces can effectively undermine Islamism".

Abu Khawla (Muhammad Bechri), human
rights activist and former chair of the
Tunisian section of Amnesty International,
(www.metransparent.com, 2/1/05)

"Egypt's rulers are afraid of peace, since peace pushes us towards democracy, and they are not interested in that. Nor are they interested in our becoming acquainted with the cultural reality which Israel has created, or with the democracy that the Israelis, together with the Jews, have implemented".

Muhammid Farid Hassanein, former member of
the Egyptian parliament, in interview with Kul Al-'Arab,
independent Israeli Arab weekly, February 2005
(www.virtualjerusalem.com)

WORLD VIEWS

"The Arab Human Development Report of 2003 states that the main impediments to Arab development are: lack of freedom. The report finds that the regional Freedom Index was at its lowest in the 90s, and that the indexes for accountability and corruption were the worst in the entire world; absence of women's empowerment; and weak human capacity (or low levels of knowledge)".

United Nations Development Programme, 2003:
(www.undp.org)

"Video games attract young to Hizbollah".

Toby Harnden in Beirut, The Daily Telegraph, 21/2/04

"The root cause of violence, poverty and division in the Middle East is not a failure to solve the peace process. The failure of the peace process stems from the continuing addiction of so many of the Arab world's leaders to fomenting violence, presiding over poverty and indulging in the politics of division".

Michael Gove, The Times, 9/11/04

23.
Jews

"The master-stroke of the Jew was to claim the leadership of the fourth estate: he founded the Movement both of the Social Democrats and the Communists. His policy was twofold: he had his 'apostles' in both political camps. Amongst the parties of the Right he encouraged those features which were most repugnant to the people. Foreign peoples, foreign workmen build him his temples, it is foreigners who create and work for him: it is foreigners who shed their blood for him. He knows no 'people's army': he has only hired mercenaries who are ready to go to death on his behalf".

Adolf Hitler, 1922
(Australasian Blackboard Community: www.abbc.net)

"Today the Jews rule this world by proxy. They get others to fight and die for them...They invented and successfully promoted Socialism, Communism, human rights and democracy so that persecuting them would appear to be wrong, so they may enjoy equal rights with others. With these they have now gained control of the most powerful countries and they, this tiny community, have become a world power".

"Treaty Now, Triumph Later - the Jews Are Making Mistakes",
Malaysian PM, Datuk Seri Dr Mahathir Mohammad, at
the10th Session of Islamic Summit Conference, 16/10/03
(Independent Media Review Analysis: www.imra.org.il)

"You shall continue to fight the Jews, and they will fight you, until the Muslims will kill them".

Sheikh Yusef Al Qaradawi, quoting from the
Hadith of Ibn-Omar and the Hadith of Abu-Hurairah,
(Middle East Media Research Institute: www.memri.org)

"From a historical perspective, what Hitler did to the Jews is exactly what they deserve. Still, we would have wished that he could have finished incinerating all the Jews in the world, but time ran out on him and therefore Allah's curse be on him and on them".

Khaled al-Zahraya from Saudi Arabia,
in the visitors book at an exhibition of photographs from
the holocaust in the Slovak town Banska Bystrica, 7/9/03
(The Jerusalem Report, 29/01/04: www.jrep.com)

"The Jews are beasts who one is entitled to kill by whatever means available".

Translation of the monthly al-Shuhada by Muhammad
Khalifa al-Tunis, issue no.44, November/December 2001,
by the Political Indoctrination Apparatus of the
Palestinian Border Guard in the Gaza strip,
taken from edition published in Egypt in 1976.

"O God, destroy the Jews and their supporters".

Prayer of Imam Shayhk Ibrahim al-Mudayris,
sermon broadcast by Gaza Palestine Satellite Channel TV,
official station of the P.A. and Gaza Voice of Palestine 1/11/02
(www.freerepublic.com)

"What's going on in the Islamic world today, and I say this with painful honesty, is actually Jew-bashing".

"The Trouble with Islam: a Muslim's call
for Reform in her Faith" by Irshad Manji,
St Martin's, 2003

WORLD VIEW

To a question about Zionism: "When people criticise Zionists they mean Jews. You are talking anti-Semitism".

Martin Luther King, Harvard University, 1968
(www.jewish-history.com/mlk.html)

24.

After Arafat

"Article 12. The complete liberation of Palestine and eradication of Zionist economic, political, military and cultural existence".

Article 19. This armed struggle will not cease unless the Zionist state [Israel] is demolished".

Fatah constitution, written in 1964,
but still on its web site, February 2005
(www.mididleeastfacts.com)

"It is not our culture to wish someone's death, but politically speaking [the death of Palestinian Authority Chairman Arafat] is not a big loss for the Palestinian people".

Fahed Fanek, Jordanian political analyst
and daily columnist, Al-Rai Newspaper
(The Jerusalem Post, October 2004)

"First and foremost, although I hate Sharon, I have to admit, after Arafat's death, that Sharon's position towards Arafat was correct: True, Yasser Arafat was responsible for the armed operations. Perhaps I wasn't brave enough to say so before - because I feared for Yasser Arafat's life - but the smuggling of the Karyn A weapons ship by Fuwad Al-Shobaki, who is still languishing unjustly in the Jericho prison, establishing the Al-Aqsa brigades, firing Jibril Rajoub and Muhammad Dahlan for disagreeing with him on the armed struggle, his alliance with Hamas, have all justified Sharon's logic and his hostility to President Arafat. Yes, Yasser Arafat supported the armed struggle and the armed intifada".

Hamada Farana, former Jordanian MP and a
member of the Palestinian National Council,
in an interview with ANB TV (London) 22/11/04,
(www.memritv.org/Transcript.asp?P1 =376)

"Hamas has announced that it accepts a Palestinian independent state within the 1967 borders with a long-term truce....For us a truce means that two warring parties live side by side in peace and security for a certain period and this period is eligible for renewal".

Sheikh Hassan Yousef, top Hamas leader
in West Bank, to Associated Press, 3/12/04
(www.icej.org)

"I think if they [Palestinians] can't achieve progress in the time of the current [Israeli] prime minister, it will be very difficult to make any progress in peace. He [Sharon] is capable of pursuing peace, and he is capable of reaching solutions, if he wants to....Israel's prime minister said he was ready to do what the Palestinians want, to facilitate the elections, and help in removing the checkpoints. He only asks for one thing: the end of the explosions, so they can work together on a solid basis."

Hosni Mubarak, Egyptian President,
Haaretz, 3/12/04

"We must respect the human mind, recognize the 'other,' respect his humanity, and show tolerance to him".

Muhammad Jammal Abu Hunud, Preacher,
in Friday sermon from the Presidency Mosque,
Gaza, and broadcast on Palestinian TV
(www.memritv.org, clip 824, 7/12/04)

"We do not encourage our sons to die. We encourage them to Shahada [martyrdom] for the homeland, for Allah. We don't say to the mothers of the Shahids, 'We have come to comfort you', but 'We have come to bless you on the wedding of your son, on the Shahada of your son. Congratulations to you on the Shahada' . . . For us, the mourning is joyous. We give out drinks, we give out sweets. Praise to God, the mourning is a joyous occasion".

Um Al-Ajrami, a Palestinian mother of a
'Shahid', in an interview on PATV, 17/12/04,
(www.pmw.org.il)

"Our people have opted for democracy as a way of life from which we will not abdicate. And we will pursue in this path, the democratic path, without any compromise".

Mahmoud Abbas, interim PLO leader,
at a Press conference in Ramallah on 22/12/04
(www.bicom.org.uk, 23/12/04)

"[There are] 300 Million Arabs, while Israel has only the sea behind it...At this stage there will be two states. Many years from now there will be only one."

Farouq Qaddumi, Fatah Leader
(www.memri.org, clip 390, December 2004)

"Jerusalem has been the capital of our capitals since the dawn of history, and will remain so. We won't share it with anyone".

Issam Sisalem, Palestinian Historian
(www.memri.org, clip 389, December 2004)

Nasir: "Some say that Iran is infiltrating the Palestinian ranks, as far as Gaza, through the Hizballah cadres or the Palestinian Islamic organizations in Iran.   Is this true? What do you think?"

Qaddumi: "If you say infiltration, then we welcome it because this is good.   It means that they are extending support for the Palestinians because they support the

Palestinian people and the Palestinian cause and the liberation of Palestine.   Therefore, this is truly a positive and not a negative thing.   Therefore, we welcome all the Arab and Islamic countries to come and infiltrate us with such support".

Farouq Qaddumi, Foreign minister of the state of Palestine and Fatah Movement Chairman, interviewed by Abbas Nasssir in Teheran, on Doha Al-Jazirah Satellite Chanel Television, an independent TV station financed by the Qatari government, broadcast on 20/12/04 (www.imra.net,il, 28/12/04)

"The greatest misconception of the West is that their culture and democracy   is indestructible and that the forces of terror and evil are not all that significant, but the bottom line is that many Muslims have their eyes set to Islamize America and the West and will not let go even after 9/11".

Nonie Darwish, an Arab who grew up in the Middle East, interview in The Jerusalem Post, 27/12/04

"We fight when we think fighting is worthwhile, and we stop fighting when it isn't. We may refrain from fighting for even a month, and then resume the resistance... We seize opportunities. We hit and run. We run! This is the way we minimize our losses".

Farouq Qaddumi, Fatah Leader, PATV, 22/12/04 (www.memritv.org, clip 438)

"At the Camp David summit [in 2000], the Palestinian leadership rejected an Israeli proposal to share sovereignty over the Aqsa Mosque. They wanted to give the Muslims all what is above the mosque, while Israel would control what's under it. We continue to reject this offer. We cannot compromise on Jerusalem".

Mahmoud Abbas,
(www.imra.org.il, 28/12/04)

"Palestinians do not feel that their living conditions improve and this cannot happen without stopping the attacks against Israel."

Article by Thaer Abu Baker, in Jordan Times, 16/1/05
(www.middleeastwindow.com, 17/1/05)

"The decision has been made to put members of the al-Aqsa Brigades in the Palestinian security services....Abu Mazen [Abbas] told us that this must happen as soon as possible....The committee gave its full support to Abu Mazen's inauguration speech to stop all military acts that harm our national interest".

Ram Allah, a PLO official, to AFP
(www.imra.org.il, 17/1/05)

"[Sharon] expects the PA to do everything for him by 'eliminating the sources of terror' or by declaring a unilateral truce. In short, any ceasefire is an exclusive Palestinian responsibility. This implies that Palestinian 'terrorism' is the cause and Israeli repression the result".

Azmi Bishara, Member of Israeli Knesset,
Al-Ahram Weekly, 13-19/1/05
(www.imra.org.il, 19/1/05)

"Our willingness to return to the 1967 borders does not mean that we have given up on the land of Palestine....We might be able to use diplomacy in order to return to the 1967 borders, but we shall not be able to use diplomacy in order to return to the 1948 borders. No one on this earth recognizes [our right to] the 1948 borders [before Israel's existence]. Therefore we shall return to the 1967 borders, but it does not mean that we have given up on Jerusalem and Haifa, Jaffa, Lod, Ramla, Natanya and Tel Aviv. We shall return to every village".

Ibrahim Mudyris, Preacher, Friday sermon on
Palestinian Authority television, 4/2/05
(www.pmw.org.il, 8/2/05)

"The Palestinians desire peace and anybody who commits violence now will be considered to be committing terrorism. We desire freedom and we desire peace. We established a hudna with Hamas, Islamic Jihad and the forces of the left and anyone who carries out an operation now is doing it on his own. This means that anyone who does something like this is a terrorist and his actions are terror".

Abdul Karim Musalam (Abu Salah),
member of Palestinian Legislative Council, interview
with IMRA, 8/2/05, translated by Michael Widlanski
(www.imra.org.il)

"We have more than five million refugees and we know that not all can return. Many probably do not want to return because they have a nice life in America or are happy in Jordan".

Mahmoud Abbas, in interview with Der Spiegel,
Ramallah, 20/2/05, published on 21/2/05,
(www.imra.org.il)

"People will throw flowers, not stones". *[on Israel's withdrawal from Gaza]*

Mahmoud Abbas, in interview with Der Spiegel,
Ramallah, 20/2/05
(www.arabnews.com)

"I have seen the democracy among the Jews, and I know that the Arabs have many legitimate demands, which we will demand in the future from the Israeli government and Israeli people.   However when I compare the living conditions of Israeli Arabs to my own living conditions, I realize that the Israeli Arabs are more fortunate than me".

Muhammid Farid Hassanein, former member of the
Egyptian parliament, in interview with Kul Al-'Arab,
Israel Arab weekly, February 2005
(www.virtualjerusalem.com)

"This is the first action that no-one is happy about. Everyone felt that the timing is not [right] and there is absolutely no need for it...It is not because resistance against the occupation is a mistake, but because the nature, location and timing of the action are a mistake".

Hassan Asfour, member of PA parliament,
on the suicide bombing in Tel Aviv which killed
and maimed tens of Israelis, on PA TV, 28/2/05
(www.pmw.org.il, 3/3/05)

"What was agreed upon today is calm until the end of this year as a maximum period of time to exchange for an Israeli commitment to withdrawal from cities and [to] release prisoners".

Mohammad Nazzal, Hamas official, after conference
in Cairo of leaders of thirteen Palestinian factions,
Financial Times, 18/3/05
(www.news.ft.com)

"It is the right of the Palestinian people to end the occupation and establish a Palestinian state with full sovereignty, with Jerusalem as its capital, and to ensure the right of Palestinians to return to their homes and property".

Six-point document, agreed by all thirteen
representatives of Palestinan factions including
Mahmoud Abbas, after conference in Cairo, presented
by Omar Suleiman, Egyptian intelligence officer, 18/3/05
(www.bicom.org.uk)

"Saturday March 19th is the end of the honeymoon period that we have given to Israel. We reject completely the result of the Cairo conference, since we did not participate...I say to the residents of Sderot: you'd better prepare your bomb shelters. You've never seen what we've got in store for you".

Mohammad Abdelal (Abu Abir), spokesman for the
Gaza-based Popular Resistance Committee, in
interview with Ynet, the website of Yedioth Achronoth
(Yedioth Achronoth, 3/18/05)

"We want the Arab nations not to normalize relations with Israel instead of exerting pressure on us and calling on Palestinians to be more flexible".

Farouk Al-Qaddoumi, Fatah leader and head
of PLO political department, to AFP, 19/3/05
(www.imra.org.il, 20/3/05)

WORLD VIEWS

"The way that the debate has gone shows how such debates often go in the House: people pay lip service to acts of terrorism by the Palestinians and then devote the majority of their speech to attacking Israel and apportioning all the blame to it....Whenever people such as Mohammad Dahlan and Jibril Rijoub attempted to crack down on terror in Gaza and the west bank, they were undermined by Yasser Arafat. That is why Mr. Dahlan resigned when Abu Mazen left - he was despairing that every time that he tried to crack down on terror, he was undermined by the leadership of the Palestinian Authority".

David Cairns. MP, in House of Commons
debate on Queen's speech, November 2004
(www.publications.parliament.uk)

"There is not going to be successful negotiations or peace without an end to terrorism. The world is changed in these past few year".

Tony Blair, British Prime Minster
(icej, 22/12/04)

"[Mahmoud Abbas] is making progress. For the time being he has managed to achieve a cessation of violence...There is a temporary neutralization of terrorist activities against Israel. It's not enough. The final result has to be a situation in which terrorism completely disappears from the area of activities that receive any kind of understanding and tolerance.

"Palestinian radicals must understand that here there are two sides with legitimate claims whose resolution requires compromise".

Ramiro Cibrian-Uzal, EU Ambassador to Israel,
Jerusalem Post 21/3/05
(www.bicom.org.uk)

"Any action constitutes terrorism if it is intended to cause death or serious bodily harm to civilians or non-combatants with the purpose of intimidating a population or compelling a government or an international organization to do or abstain from doing any act".

Kofi Annan, UN Secretary General, in his report
'In Larger Freedom', endorsed by a high-level panel,
UN News Centre, 21/3/05
(www.bicom.org.uk, 22/3/05)

Appendix

Appendix A

Balfour Declaration, 1917

Foreign Office, November 2nd, 1917.

Dear Lord Rothschild,

I have much pleasure in conveying to you, on behalf of His Majesty's Government, the following declaration of sympathy with Jewish Zionist aspirations which has been submitted to, and approved by, the Cabinet.

"His Majesty's Government view with favour the establishment in Palestine of a national home for the Jewish people, and will use their best endeavours to facilitate the achievement of the object, it being clearly understood that nothing shall be done which may prejudice the civil and religious' rights of existing non-Jewish communities in Palestine, or the rights and political status enjoyed by Jews in any other country".

I should be grateful if you would bring this declaration to the knowledge of the Zionist Federation.

Yours sincerely,

(Signed) Arthur James Balfour

Appendix B

British Mandate for Palestine, 1922

C. 529. M. 314. 1922. VI.

**Communiqué au Conseil et aux
Membres de la Société**

Genève, le 12 août 1922.

SOCIÉTÉ DES NATIONS

———

MANDAT POUR LA PALESTINE

————

LEAGUE OF NATIONS

———

MANDATE FOR PALESTINE

———

LEAGUE OF NATIONS*

MANDATE FOR PALESTINE

The Council of the League of Nations:

Whereas the Principal Allied Powers have agreed, for the purpose of giving effect to the provisions of Article 22 of the Covenant of the League of Nations, to entrust to a Mandatory selected by the said Powers the administration of the territory of Palestine, which formerly belonged to the Turkish Empire, within such boundaries as may be fixed by them; and

Whereas the Principal Allied Powers have also agreed that the Mandatory should be responsible for putting into effect the declaration originally made on November 2nd, 1917, by the Government of His Britannic Majesty, and adopted by the said Powers, in favour of the establishment in Palestine of a national home for the Jewish people, it being clearly understood that nothing should be done which might prejudice the civil and religious rights of existing non-Jewish communities in Palestine, or the rights and political status enjoyed by Jews in any other country; and

Whereas recognition has thereby been given to the historical connection of the Jewish people with Palestine and to the grounds for reconstituting their national home in that country; and

Whereas the Principal Allied Powers have selected His Britannic Majesty as the Mandatory for Palestine; and

Whereas the mandate in respect of Palestine has been formulated in the following terms and submitted to the Council of the League for approval; and

Whereas His Britannic Majesty has accepted the mandate in respect of Palestine and undertaken to exercise it on behalf of the League of Nations in conformity with the following provisions; and

Whereas by the aforementioned Article 22 (paragraph 8), it is provided that the degree of authority, control or administration to be exercised by the Mandatory, not having been previously agreed upon by the Members of the League, shall be explicitly defined by the Council of the League of Nations;

Confirming the said mandate, defines its terms as follows:

Article 1
The Mandatory shall have full powers of legislation and of administration, save as they may be limited by the terms of this mandate.

Article 2
The Mandatory shall be responsible for placing the country under such political, administrative and economic conditions as will secure the establishment of the Jewish national home, as laid down in the preamble, and the development of self-governing institutions, and also for safeguarding the civil and religious rights of all the inhabitants of Palestine, irrespective of race and religion.

Article 3
The Mandatory shall, so far as circumstances permit, encourage local autonomy.

Article 4
An appropriate Jewish agency shall be recognised as a public body for the purpose of advising and co-operating with the Administration of Palestine in such economic, social and other matters as may affect the establishment of the Jewish national home and the interests of the Jewish population in Palestine, and, subject always to the control of the Administration, to assist and take part in the development of the country.

The Zionist Organisation, so long as its organisation and constitution are in the opinion of the Mandatory appropriate, shall be recognised as such agency. It shall take steps in consultation with His Britannic Majesty's Government to secure the co-operation of all Jews who are willing to assist in the establishment of the Jewish national home.

Article 5
The Mandatory shall be responsible for seeing that no Palestine territory shall be ceded or leased to, or in any way placed under the control of, the Government of any foreign Power.

Article 6

The Administration of Palestine, while ensuring that the rights and position of other sections of the population are not prejudiced, shall facilitate Jewish immigration under suitable conditions and shall encourage, in co-operation with the Jewish agency referred to in Article 4, close settlement by Jews on the land, including State lands and waste lands not required for public purposes.

Article 7

The Administration of Palestine shall be responsible for enacting a nationality law. There shall be included in this law provisions framed so as to facilitate the acquisition of Palestinian citizenship by Jews who take up their permanent residence in Palestine.

Article 8

The privileges and immunities of foreigners, including the benefits of consular jurisdiction and protection as formerly enjoyed by Capitulation or usage in the Ottoman Empire, shad not be applicable in Palestine.

Unless the Powers whose nationals enjoyed the afore-mentioned privileges and immunities on August 1st, 1914, shall have previously renounced the right to their re-establishment, or shall have agreed to their non-application for a specified period, these privileges and immunities shall, at the expiration of the mandate, be immediately reestablished in their entirety or with such modifications as may have been agreed upon between the Powers concerned.

Article 9

The Mandatory shall be responsible for seeing that the judicial system established in Palestine shall assure to foreigners, as well as to natives, a complete guarantee of their rights.

Respect for the personal status of the various peoples and communities and for their religious interests shall be fully guaranteed. In particular, the control and administration of Wakfs shall be exercised in accordance with religious law and the dispositions of the founders.

Article 10

Pending the making of special extradition agreements relating to Palestine, the extradition treaties in force between the Mandatory and other foreign Powers shall apply to Palestine.

Article 11

The Administration of Palestine shall take all necessary measures to safeguard the interests of the community in connection with the development of the country, and, subject to any international obligations accepted by the Mandatory, shall have full power to provide for public ownership or control of any of the natural resources of the country or of the public works, services and utilities established or to be established therein. It shall introduce a land system appropriate to the needs of the country, having regard, among other things, to the desirability of promoting the close settlement and intensive cultivation of the land.

The Administration may arrange with the Jewish agency mentioned in Article 4 to construct or operate, upon fair and equitable terms, any public works, services and utilities, and to develop any of the natural resources of the country, in so far as these matters are not directly undertaken by the Administration. Any such arrangements shall provide that no profits distributed by such agency, directly or indirectly, shall exceed a reasonable rate of interest on the capital, and any further profits shall be utilised by it for the benefit of the country in a manner approved by the Administration.

Article 12

The Mandatory shall be entrusted with the control of the foreign relations of Palestine and the right to issue exequaturs to consuls appointed by foreign Powers. He shall also be entitled to afford diplomatic and consular protection to citizens of Palestine when outside its territorial limit.

Article 13

All responsibility in connection with the Holy Places and religious buildings or sites in Palestine, including that of preserving existing rights and of securing free access to the Holy Places, religious buildings and sites and the free exercise of worship, while ensuring the requirements of public order and decorum, is assumed by the Mandatory, who shall be responsible solely to the League of Nations in all matters connected herewith, provided that nothing in this article shall prevent the Mandatory from entering into such arrangements as he may deem reasonable with the Administration for the purpose of carrying the provisions of this article into effect; and provided also that nothing in this mandate shah be construed as conferring upon the Mandatory authority to interfere with the fabric or the management of purely Moslem sacred shrines, the immunities of which are guaranteed.

Article 14

A special Commission shall be appointed by the Mandatory to study, define and determine the rights and claims in connection with the Holy Places and the rights and claims relating to the different religious communities in Palestine. The method of nomination, the composition and the functions of this Commission shall be submitted to the Council of the League for its approval, and the Commission shall not be appointed or enter upon its functions without the approval of the Council.

Article 15

The Mandatory shall see that complete freedom of conscience and the free exercise of all forms of worship, subject only to the maintenance of public order and morals, are ensured to all. No discrimination of any kind shall be made between the inhabitants of Palestine on the ground of race, religion or language. No person shall be excluded from Palestine on the sole ground of his religious belief.

The right of each community to maintain its own schools for the education of its own members in its own language, while conforming to such educational requirements of a general nature as the Administration may impose, shall not be denied or impaired.

Article 16

The Mandatory shall be responsible for exercising such supervision over religious or eleemosynary bodies of all faiths in Palestine as may be required for the maintenance of public order and good government. Subject to such supervision, no measures shall be taken in Palestine to obstruct or interfere with the enterprise of such bodies or to discriminate against any representative or member of them on the ground of his religion or nationality.

Article 17

The Administration of Palestine may organise on a voluntary basis the forces necessary for the preservation of peace and order, and also for the defence of the country, subject, however, to the supervision of the Mandatory, but shall not use them for purposes other than those above specified save with the consent of the Mandatory. Except for such purposes, no military, naval or air forces shall be raised or maintained by the Administration of Palestine.

Nothing in this article shall preclude the Administration of Palestine from contributing to the cost of the maintenance of the forces of the Mandatory in Palestine.

The Mandatory shall be entitled at all times to use the roads; railways and ports of Palestine for the movement of armed forces and the carriage of fuel and supplies.

Article 18

The Mandatory shall see that there is no discrimination in Palestine against the nationals of any State Member of the League of Nations (including companies incorporated under its laws) as compared with those of the Mandatory or of any foreign State in matters concerning taxation, commerce or navigation, the exercise of industries or professions, or in the treatment of merchant vessels or civil aircraft. Similarly, there shall be no discrimination in Palestine against goods originating in or destined for any of the said States, and there shall be freedom of transit under equitable conditions across the mandated area.

Subject as aforesaid and to the other provisions of this mandate, the Administration of Palestine may, on the advice of the Mandatory, impose such taxes and customs duties as it may consider necessary and take such steps as it may think best to promote the development of the natural resources of the country and to safeguard the interests of the population. It may also, on the advice of the Mandatory, conclude a special customs agreement with any State the territory of which in 1914 was wholly included in Asiatic Turkey or Arabia.

Article 19

The Mandatory shall adhere on behalf of the Administration of Palestine to any general international conventions already existing, or which may be concluded hereafter with the approval of the League of Nations, respecting the slave traffic, the traffic in arms and ammunition, or the traffic in drugs, or relating to commercial equality, freedom of transit and navigation, aerial navigation and postal, telegraphic and wireless communication or literary, artistic or industrial property.

Article 20

The Mandatory shall co-operate on behalf of the Administration of Palestine, so far as religious, social and other conditions may permit, in the execution of any common policy adopted by the League of nations for preventing and combating disease, including diseases of plants and animals.

Article 21

The Mandatory shall secure the enactment within twelve months from this date, and shall ensure the execution of a Law of Antiquities based on the following rules. This law shall ensure equality of treatment in the matter of excavations and archaeological research to the nationals of all States Members of the League of Nations.

(1)

"Antiquity" means any construction or any product of human activity earlier than the year 1700 A.D.

(2)

The law for the protection of antiquities shall proceed by encouragement rather than by threat.

Any person who, having discovered an antiquity without being furnished with the authorisation referred to in paragraph 5, reports the same to an official of the competent Department, shall be rewarded according to the value of the discovery.

(3)

No antiquity may be disposed of except to the competent Department, unless this Department renounces the acquisition of any such antiquity.

No antiquity may leave the country without an export licence from the said Department.

(4)

Any person who maliciously or negligently destroys or damages an antiquity shall be liable to a penalty to be fixed.

(5)

No clearing of ground or digging with the object of finding antiquities shall be permitted, under penalty of fine, except to persons authorised by the competent Department.

(6)

Equitable terms shall be fixed for expropriation, temporary or permanent, of lands which might be of historical or archaeological interest.

(7)

Authorisation to excavate shall only be granted to persons who show sufficient guarantees of archaeological experience. The Administration of Palestine shall not, in granting these authorisations, act in such a way as to exclude scholars of any nation without good grounds.

(8)

The proceeds of excavations may be divided between the excavator and the competent Department in a proportion fixed by that Department. If division seems impossible for scientific reasons, the excavator shall receive a fair indemnity in lieu of a part of the find.

Article 22

English, Arabic and Hebrew shall be the official languages of Palestine. Any statement or inscription in Arabic on stamps or money in Palestine shall be repeated in Hebrew and any statement or inscription in Hebrew shall be repeated in Arabic.

Article 23

The Administration of Palestine shall recognise the holy days of the respective communities in Palestine as legal days of rest for the members of such communities.

Article 24

The Mandatory shall make to the Council of the League of Nations an annual report to the satisfaction of the Council as to the measures taken during the year to carry out the provisions of the mandate. Copies of all laws and regulations promulgated or issued during the year shall be communicated with the report.

Article 25

In the territories lying between the Jordan and the eastern boundary of Palestine as ultimately determined, the Mandatory shall be entitled, with the consent of the Council of the League of Nations, to postpone or withhold application of such provisions of this mandate as he may consider inapplicable to the existing local conditions, and to make such provision for the administration of the territories as he may consider suitable to those conditions, provided that no action shall be taken which is inconsistent with the provisions of Articles 15, 16 and 18.

Article 26

The Mandatory agrees that, if any dispute whatever should arise between e Mandatory and another Member of the League of Nations relating to the interpretation or the application of the provisions of the mandate, such dispute, if it cannot be settled by negotiation, shall be submitted to the Permanent Court of International Justice provided for by Article 14 of the Covenant of the League of Nations.

Article 27

The consent of the Council of the League of Nations is required for any modification of the terms of this mandate.

Article 28

In the event of the termination of the mandate hereby conferred upon the Mandatory, the Council of the League of Nations shall make such arrangements as may be deemed necessary for safeguarding in perpetuity, under guarantee of the League, the rights secured by Articles 13 and 14, and shall use its influence for securing, under the guarantee of the League, that the Government of Palestine will fully honour the financial obligations legitimately incurred by the Administration of Palestine during the period of the mandate, including the rights of public servants to pensions or gratuities.

The present instrument shall be deposited in original in the archives of the League of Nations and certified copies shall be forwarded by the Secretary-General of the League of Nations to all Members of the League.

Done at London the twenty-fourth day of July, one thousand nine hundred and twenty-two.

Certified true copy:
SECRETARY-GENERAL
* Nineteenth Session of the Council
Thirteenth Meeting
Held at St James' Palace, London on
July 24th, 1922, at 3.p.m

Appendix C, 1947

United Nations General Assembly Resolution 181, (II) (A + B)November 1947

Future government of Palestine

A

The General Assembly,

Having met in special session at the request of the mandatory Power to constitute and instruct a special committee to prepare for the consideration of the question of the future government of Palestine at the second regular session;

Having constituted a Special Committee and instructed it to investigate all questions and issues relevant to the problem of Palestine, and to prepare proposals for the solution of the problem, and

Having received and examined the report of the Special Committee (document A/364) 1/ including a number of unanimous recommendations and a plan of partition with economic union approved by the majority of the Special Committee,

Considers that the present situation in Palestine is one which is likely to impair the general welfare and friendly relations among nations;

Takes note of the declaration by the mandatory Power that it plans to complete its evacuation of Palestine by 1 August 1948;

Recommends to the United Kingdom, as the mandatory Power for Palestine, and to all other Members of the United Nations the adoption and implementation, with regard to the future government of Palestine, of the Plan of Partition with Economic Union set out below;

Requests that

(a) The Security Council take the necessary measures as provided for in the plan for its implementation;

(b) The Security Council consider, if circumstances during the transitional period require such consideration, whether the situation in Palestine constitutes a threat to the peace. If it decides that such a threat exists, and in order to maintain international peace and security, the Security Council should supplement the authorization of the General Assembly by taking measures, under Articles 39 and 41 of the Charter, to empower the United Nations Commission, as provided in this resolution, to exercise in Palestine the functions which are assigned to it by this resolution;

(c) The Security Council determine as a threat to the peace, breach of the peace or act of aggression, in accordance with Article 39 of the Charter, any attempt to alter by force the settlement envisaged by this resolution;

(d) The Trusteeship Council be informed of the responsibilities envisaged for it in this plan;

Calls upon the inhabitants of Palestine to take such steps as may be necessary on their part to put this plan into effect;

Appeals to all Governments and all peoples to refrain from taking action which might hamper or delay the carrying out of these recommendations, and

Authorizes the Secretary-General to reimburse travel and subsistence expenses of the members of the Commission referred to in Part I, Section B, paragraph 1 below, on such basis and in such form as he may determine most appropriate in the circumstances, and to provide the Commission with the necessary staff to assist in carrying out the functions assigned to the Commission by the General Assembly.

B 2/

The General Assembly

Authorizes the Secretary-General to draw from the Working Capital Fund a sum not to exceed $2,000,000 for the purposes set forth in the last paragraph of the resolution on the future government of Palestine.

Hundred and twenty-eighth plenary meeting
29 November 1947

[At its hundred and twenty-eighth plenary meeting on 29 November 1947 the General Assembly, in accordance with the terms of the above resolution [181 A], elected the following members of the United Nations Commission on Palestine: **Bolivia, Czechoslovakia, Denmark, Panama and Philippines.]**

PLAN OF PARTITION WITH ECONOMIC UNION

PART I
Future constitution and government of Palestine

A. TERMINATION OF MANDATE, PARTITION AND INDEPENDENCE

1. The Mandate for Palestine shall terminate as soon as possible but in any case not later than 1 August 1948.

2. The armed forces of the mandatory Power shall be progressively withdrawn from Palestine, the withdrawal to be completed as soon as possible but in any case not later than 1 August 1948.

The mandatory Power shall advise the Commission, as far in advance as possible, of its intention to terminate the Mandate and to evacuate each area.

The mandatory Power shall use its best endeavours to ensure than an area situated in the territory of the Jewish State, including a seaport and hinterland adequate to provide facilities for a substantial immigration, shall be evacuated at the earliest possible date and in any event not later than 1 February 1948.

3. Independent Arab and Jewish States and the Special International Regime for the City of Jerusalem, set forth in part III of this plan, shall come into existence in Palestine two months after the evacuation of the armed forces of the mandatory Power has been completed but in any case not later than 1 October 1948. The boundaries of the Arab State, the Jewish State, and the City of Jerusalem shall be as described in parts II and III below.

4. The period between the adoption by the General Assembly of its recommendation on the question of Palestine and the establishment of the independence of the Arab and Jewish States shall be a transitional period.

B. STEPS PREPARATORY TO INDEPENDENCE

1. A Commission shall be set up consisting of one representative of each of five Member States. The Members represented on the Commission shall be elected by the General Assembly on as broad a basis, geographically and otherwise, as possible.

2. The administration of Palestine shall, as the mandatory Power withdraws its armed forces, be progressively turned over to the Commission; which shall act in conformity with the recommendations of the General Assembly, under the guidance of the Security Council. The mandatory Power shall to the fullest possible extent co-ordinate its plans for withdrawal with the plans of the Commission to take over and administer areas which have been evacuated.

In the discharge of this administrative responsibility the Commission shall have authority to issue necessary regulations and take other measures as required.

The mandatory Power shall not take any action to prevent, obstruct or delay the implementation by the Commission of the measures recommended by the General Assembly.

3. On its arrival in Palestine the Commission shall proceed to carry out measures for the establishment of the frontiers of the Arab and Jewish States and the City of Jerusalem in accordance with the general lines of the recommendations of the General Assembly on the partition of

Palestine. Nevertheless, the boundaries as described in part II of this plan are to be modified in such a way that village areas as a rule will not be divided by state boundaries unless pressing reasons make that necessary.

4. The Commission, after consultation with the democratic parties and other public organizations of The Arab and Jewish States, shall select and establish in each State as rapidly as possible a Provisional Council of Government. The activities of both the Arab and Jewish Provisional Councils of Government shall be carried out under the general direction of the Commission.

If by 1 April 1948 a Provisional Council of Government cannot be selected for either of the States, or, if selected, cannot carry out its functions, the Commission shall communicate that fact to the Security Council for such action with respect to that State as the Security Council may deem proper, and to the Secretary-General for communication to the Members of the United Nations.

5. Subject to the provisions of these recommendations, during the transitional period the Provisional Councils of Government, acting under the Commission, shall have full authority in the areas under their control, including authority over matters of immigration and land regulation.

6. The Provisional Council of Government of each State acting under the Commission, shall progressively receive from the Commission full responsibility for the administration of that State in the period between the termination of the Mandate and the establishment of the State's independence.

7. The Commission shall instruct the Provisional Councils of Government of both the Arab and Jewish States, after their formation, to proceed to the establishment of administrative organs of government, central and local.

8. The Provisional Council of Government of each State shall, within the shortest time possible, recruit an armed militia from the residents of that State, sufficient in number to maintain internal order and to prevent frontier clashes.

This armed militia in each State shall, for operational purposes, be under the command of Jewish or Arab officers resident in that State, but general political and military control, including the choice of the militia's High Command, shall be exercised by the Commission.

9. The Provisional Council of Government of each State shall, not later than two months after the withdrawal of the armed forces of the mandatory Power, hold elections to the Constituent Assembly which shall be conducted on democratic lines.

The election regulations in each State shall be drawn up by the Provisional Council of Government and approved by the Commission. Qualified voters for each State for this election shall be persons over eighteen years of age who are: (a) Palestinian citizens residing in that State and (b) Arabs and Jews residing in the State, although not Palestinian citizens, who, before voting, have signed a notice of intention to become citizens of such State.

Arabs and Jews residing in the City of Jerusalem who have signed a notice of intention to become citizens, the Arabs of the Arab State and the Jews of the Jewish State, shall be entitled to vote in the Arab and Jewish States respectively.

Women may vote and be elected to the Constituent Assemblies.

During the transitional period no Jew shall be permitted to establish residence in the area of the proposed Arab State, and no Arab shall be permitted to establish residence in the area of the proposed Jewish State, except by special leave of the Commission.

10. The Constituent Assembly of each State shall draft a democratic constitution for its State and choose a provisional government to succeed the Provisional Council of Government appointed by the Commission. The constitutions of the States shall embody chapters 1 and 2 of the Declaration provided for in section C below and include inter alia provisions for:

(a) Establishing in each State a legislative body elected by universal suffrage and by secret ballot on the basis of proportional representation, and an executive body responsible to the legislature;

(b) Settling all international disputes in which the State may be involved by peaceful means in such a manner that international peace and security, and justice, are not endangered;

(c) Accepting the obligation of the State to refrain in its international relations from the threat or use of force against the territorial integrity of political independence of any State, or in any other manner inconsistent with the purposes of the United Nations;

(d) Guaranteeing to all persons equal and non-discriminatory rights in civil, political, economic and religious matters and the enjoyment of human rights and fundamental freedoms, including freedom of religion, language, speech and publication, education, assembly and association;

(e) Preserving freedom of transit and visit for all residents and citizens of the other State in Palestine and the City of Jerusalem, subject to considerations of national security, provided that each State shall control residence within its borders.

11. The Commission shall appoint a preparatory economic commission of three members to make whatever arrangements are possible for economic co-operation, with a view to establishing, as soon as practicable, the Economic Union and the Joint Economic Board, as provided in section D below.

12. During the period between the adoption of the recommendations on the question of Palestine by the General Assembly and the termination of the Mandate, the mandatory Power in Palestine shall maintain full responsibility for administration in areas from which it has not withdrawn its armed forces. The Commission shall assist the mandatory Power in the carrying out of these functions. Similarly the mandatory Power shall co-operate with the Commission in the execution of its functions.

13. With a view to ensuring that there shall be continuity in the functioning of administrative services and that, on the withdrawal of the armed forces of the mandatory Power, the whole administration shall be in the charge of the Provisional Councils and the Joint Economic Board, respectively, acting under the Commission, there shall be a progressive transfer, from the mandatory Power to the Commission, of responsibility for all the functions of government, including that of maintaining law and order in the areas from which the forces of the mandatory Power have been withdrawn.

14. The Commission shall be guided in its activities by the recommendations of the General Assembly and by such instructions as the Security Council may consider necessary to issue.

The measures taken by the Commission, within the recommendations of the General Assembly, shall become immediately effective unless the Commission has previously received contrary instructions from the Security Council.

The Commission shall render <u>periodic monthly progress reports</u>, or more frequently if desirable, to the Security Council.

15. The Commission shall make its final report to the next regular session of the General Assembly and to the Security Council simultaneously.

C. DECLARATION

A declaration shall be made to the United Nations by the provisional government of each proposed State before independence. It shall contain inter alia the following clauses:

General Provision

The stipulations contained in the declaration are recognized as fundamental laws of the State and no law, regulation or official action shall conflict or interfere with these stipulations, nor shall any law, regulation or official action prevail over them.

Chapter 1

Holy Places, religious buildings and sites

1. Existing rights in respect of Holy Places and religious buildings or sites shall not be denied or impaired.

2. In so far as Holy Places are concerned, the liberty of access, visit and transit shall be guaranteed, in conformity with existing rights, to all residents and citizens of the other State and of the City of Jerusalem, as well as to aliens, without distinction as to nationality, subject to requirements of national security, public order and decorum.

Similarly, freedom of worship shall be guaranteed in conformity with existing rights, subject to the maintenance of public order and decorum.

3. Holy Places and religious buildings or sites shall be preserved. No act shall be permitted which may in any way impair their sacred character. If at any time it appears to the Government that any particular Holy Place, religious building or site is in need of urgent repair, the Government may call upon the community or communities concerned to carry out such repair. The Government may carry it out itself at the expense of the community or communities concerned if no action is taken within a reasonable time.

4. No taxation shall be levied in respect of any Holy Place, religious building or site which was exempt from taxation on the date of the creation of the State.

No change in the incidence of such taxation shall be made which would either discriminate between the owners or occupiers of Holy Places, religious buildings or sites, or would place such owners or occupiers in a position less favourable in relation to the general incidence of taxation than existed at the time of the adoption of the Assembly's recommendations.

5. The Governor of the City of Jerusalem shall have the right to determine whether the provisions of the Constitution of the State in relation to Holy Places, religious buildings and sites within the borders of the State and the religious rights appertaining thereto, are being properly applied and respected, and to make decisions on the basis of existing rights in cases of disputes which may arise between the different religious communities or the rites of a religious community with respect to such places, buildings and sites. He shall receive full co-operation and such privileges and immunities as are necessary for the exercise of his functions in the State.

Chapter 2

Religious and Minority Rights

1. Freedom of conscience and the free exercise of all forms of worship, subject only to the maintenance of public order and morals, shall be ensured to all.

2. No discrimination of any kind shall be made between the inhabitants on the ground of race, religion, language or sex.

3. All persons within the jurisdiction of the State shall be entitled to equal protection of the laws.

4. The family law and personal status of the various minorities and their religious interests, including endowments, shall be respected.

5. Except as may be required for the maintenance of public order and good government, no measure shall be taken to obstruct or interfere with the enterprise of religious or charitable bodies of all faiths or to discriminate against any representative or member of these bodies on the ground of his religion or nationality.

6. The State shall ensure adequate primary and secondary education for the Arab and Jewish minority, respectively, in its own language and its cultural traditions.

The right of each community to maintain its own schools for the education of its own members in its own language, while conforming to such educational requirements of a general nature as the State may impose, shall not be denied or impaired. Foreign educational establishments shall continue their activity on the basis of their existing rights.

7. No restriction shall be imposed on the free use by any citizen of the State of any language in private intercourse, in commerce, in religion, in the Press or in publications of any kind, or at public meetings.

8. No expropriation of land owned by an Arab in the Jewish State (by a Jew in the Arab State) shall be allowed except for public purposes. In all cases of expropriation full compensation as fixed by the Supreme Court shall be paid previous to dispossession.

Chapter 3

Citizenship, international conventions and financial obligations

1. Citizenship. Palestinian citizens residing in Palestine outside the

City of Jerusalem, as well as Arabs and Jews who, not holding Palestinian citizenship, reside in Palestine outside the City of Jerusalem shall, upon the recognition of independence, become citizens of the State in which they are resident and enjoy full civil and political rights. Persons over the age of eighteen years may opt, within one year from the date of recognition of independence of the State in which they reside, for citizenship of the other State, providing that no Arab residing in the area of the proposed Arab State shall have the right to opt for citizenship in the proposed Jewish State and no Jew residing in the proposed Jewish State shall have the right to opt for citizenship in the proposed Arab State. The exercise of this right of option will be taken to include the wives and children under eighteen years of age of persons so opting.

Arabs residing in the area of the proposed Jewish State and Jews residing in the area of the proposed Arab State who have signed a notice of intention to opt for citizenship of the other State shall be eligible to vote in the elections to the Constituent Assembly of that State, but not in the elections to the Constituent Assembly of the State in which they reside.

2. International conventions. (a) The State shall be bound by all the international agreements and conventions, both general and special, to which Palestine has become a party. Subject to any right of denunciation provided for therein, such agreements and conventions shall be respected by the State throughout the period for which they were concluded.

(b) Any dispute about the applicability and continued validity of international conventions or treaties signed or adhered to by the mandatory Power on behalf of Palestine shall be referred to the International Court of Justice in accordance with the provisions of the Statute of the Court.

3. Financial obligations. (a) The State shall respect and fulfil all financial obligations of whatever nature assumed on behalf of Palestine by the mandatory Power during the exercise of the Mandate and recognized by the State. This provision includes the right of public servants to pensions, compensation or gratuities.

(b) These obligations shall be fulfilled through participation in the Joint economic Board in respect of those obligations applicable to

Palestine as a whole, and individually in respect of those applicable to, and fairly apportionable between, the States.

(c) A Court of Claims, affiliated with the Joint Economic Board, and composed of one member appointed by the United Nations, one representative of the United Kingdom and one representative of the State concerned, should be established. Any dispute between the United Kingdom and the State respecting claims not recognized by the latter should be referred to that Court.

(d) Commercial concessions granted in respect of any part of Palestine prior to the adoption of the resolution by the General Assembly shall continue to be valid according to their terms, unless modified by agreement between the concession-holder and the State.

Chapter 4

Miscellaneous provisions

1. The provisions of chapters 1 and 2 of the declaration shall be under the guarantee of the United Nations, and no modifications shall be made in them without the assent of the General Assembly of the United nations. Any Member of the United Nations shall have the right to bring to the attention of the General Assembly any infraction or danger of infraction of any of these stipulations, and the General Assembly may thereupon make such recommendations as it may deem proper in the circumstances.

2. Any dispute relating to the application or the interpretation of this declaration shall be referred, at the request of either party, to the International Court of Justice, unless the parties agree to another mode of settlement.

D. ECONOMIC UNION AND TRANSIT

1. The Provisional Council of Government of each State shall enter into an undertaking with respect to economic union and transit. This undertaking shall be drafted by the commission provided for in section B, paragraph 1, utilizing to the greatest possible extent the advice and co-operation of representative organizations and bodies from each of the proposed States. It shall contain provisions to establish the

Economic Union of Palestine and provide for other matters of common interest. If by 1 April 1948 the Provisional Councils of Government have not entered into the undertaking, the undertaking shall be put into force by the Commission.

The Economic Union of Palestine

2. The objectives of the Economic Union of Palestine shall be:

(a) A customs union;

(b) A joint currency system providing for a single foreign exchange rate;

(c) Operation in the common interest on a non-discriminatory basis of railways; inter-State highways; postal, telephone and telegraphic services, and port and airports involved in international trade and commerce;

(d) Joint economic development, especially in respect of irrigation, land reclamation and soil conservation;

(e) Access for both States and for the City of Jerusalem on a non-discriminatory basis to water and power facilities.

3. There shall be established a Joint Economic Board, which shall consist of three representatives of each of the two States and three foreign members appointed by the Economic and Social Council of the United Nations. The foreign members shall be appointed in the first instance for a term of three years; they shall serve as individuals and not as representatives of States.

4. The functions of the Joint Economic Board shall be to implement either directly or by delegation the measures necessary to realize the objectives of the Economic Union. It shall have all powers of organization and administration necessary to fulfil its functions.

5. The States shall bind themselves to put into effect the decisions of the Joint Economic Board. The Board's decisions shall be taken by a majority vote.

6. In the event of failure of a State to take the necessary action the

Board may, by a vote of six members, decide to withhold an appropriate portion of that part of the customs revenue to which the State in question is entitled under the Economic Union. Should the State persist in its failure to co-operate, the Board may decide by a simple majority vote upon such further sanctions, including disposition of funds which it has withheld, as it may deem appropriate.

7. In relation to economic development, the functions of the Board shall be the planning, investigation and encouragement of joint development projects, but it shall not undertake such projects except with the assent of both States and the City of Jerusalem, in the event that Jerusalem is directly involved in the development project.

8. In regard to the joint currency system the currencies circulating in the two States and the City of Jerusalem shall be issued under the authority of the Joint Economic Board, which shall be the sole issuing authority and which shall determine the reserves to be held against such currencies.

9. So far as is consistent with paragraph 2 (b) above, each State may operate its own central bank, control its own fiscal and credit policy, its foreign exchange receipts and expenditures, the grant of import licenses, and may conduct international financial operations on its own faith and credit. During the first two years after the termination of the Mandate, the Joint Economic Board shall have the authority to take such measures as may be necessary to ensure that--to the extent that the total foreign exchange revenues of the two States from the export of goods and services permit, and provided that each State takes appropriate measures to conserve its own foreign exchange resources- -each State shall have available, in any twelve months' period, foreign exchange sufficient to assure the supply of quantities of imported goods and services for consumption in its territory equivalent to the quantities of such goods and services consumed in that territory in the twelve months' period ending 31 December 1947.

10. All economic authority not specifically vested in the Joint Economic Board is reserved to each State.

11. There shall be a common customs tariff with complete freedom of trade between the States, and between the States and the City of Jerusalem.

12. The tariff schedules shall be drawn up by a Tariff Commission,

consisting of representatives of each of the States in equal numbers, and shall be submitted to the Joint Economic Board for approval by a majority vote. In case of disagreement in the Tariff Commission, the Joint Economic Board shall arbitrate the points of difference. In the event that the Tariff Commission fails to draw up any schedule by a date to be fixed, the Joint Economic Board shall determine the tariff schedule.

13. The following items shall be a first charge on the customs and other common revenue of the Joint Economic Board:

(a) The expenses of the customs service and of the operation of the joint services;

(b) The administrative expenses of the Joint Economic Board;

(c) The financial obligations of the Administration of Palestine consisting of:

(i) The service of the outstanding public debt;

(ii) The cost of superannuation benefits, now being paid or falling due in the future, in accordance with the rules and to the extent established by paragraph 3 of chapter 3 above.

14. After these obligations have been met in full, the surplus revenue from the customs and other common services shall be divided in the following manner: not less than 5 per cent and not more than 10 per cent to the City of Jerusalem; the residue shall be allocated to each State by the Joint Economic Board equitably, with the objective of maintaining a sufficient and suitable level of government and social services in each State, except that the share of either State shall not exceed the amount of that State's contribution to the revenues of the Economic Union by more than approximately four million pounds in any year. The amount granted may be adjusted by the Board according to the price level in relation to the prices prevailing at the time of the establishment of the Union. After five years, the principles of the distribution of the joint revenues may be revised by the Joint Economic Board on a basis of equity.

15. All international conventions and treaties affecting customs tariff rates, and those communications services under the jurisdiction of the

Joint Economic Board, shall be entered into by both States. In these matters, the two States shall be bound to act in accordance with the majority vote of the Joint Economic Board.

16. The Joint Economic Board shall endeavour to secure for Palestine's export fair and equal access to world markets.

17. All enterprises operated by the Joint Economic Board shall pay fair wages on a uniform basis.

Freedom of transit and visit

18. The undertaking shall contain provisions preserving freedom of transit and visit for all residents or citizens of both States and of the City of Jerusalem, subject to security considerations; provided that each state and the City shall control residence within its borders.

Termination, modification and interpretation of the undertaking

19. The undertaking and any treaty issuing therefrom shall remain in force for a period of ten years. It shall continue in force until notice of termination, to take effect two years thereafter, is given by either of the parties.

20. During the initial ten-year period, the undertaking and any treaty issuing therefrom may not be modified except by consent of both parties and with the approval of the General Assembly.

21. Any dispute relating to the application or the interpretation of the undertaking and any treaty issuing therefrom shall be referred, at the request of either party, to the international Court of Justice, unless the parties agree to another mode of settlement.

E. ASSETS

1. The movable assets of the Administration of Palestine shall be allocated to the Arab and Jewish States and the City of Jerusalem on an equitable basis. Allocations should be made by the United Nations Commission referred to in section B, paragraph 1, above. Immovable assets shall become the property of the government of the territory in which they are situated.

2. During the period between the appointment of the United Nations Commission and the termination of the Mandate, the mandatory Power shall, except in respect of ordinary operations, consult with the Commission on any measure which it may contemplate involving the liquidation, disposal or encumbering of the assets of the Palestine Government, such as the accumulated treasury surplus, the proceeds of Government bond issues, State lands or any other asset.

F. ADMISSION TO MEMBERSHIP IN THE UNITED NATIONS

When the independence of either the Arab or the Jewish State as envisaged in this plan has become effective and the declaration and undertaking, as envisaged in this plan, have been signed by either of them, sympathetic consideration should be given to its application for admission to membership in the United Nations in accordance with Article 4 of the Charter of the United Nations.

PART II

Boundaries 5/

A. THE ARAB STATE

The area of the Arab State in Western Galilee is bounded on the west by the Mediterranean and on the north by the frontier of the Lebanon from Ras en Naqura to a point north of Saliha. From there the boundary proceeds southwards, leaving the built-up area of Saliha in the Arab State, to join the southernmost point of this village. Thence it follows the western boundary line of the villages of `Alma, Rihaniya and Teitaba, thence following the northern boundary line of Meirun village to join the Acre-Safad sub-district boundary line. It follows this line to a point west of Es Sammu'i village and joins it again at the northernmost point of Farradiya. Thence it follows the sub-district boundary line to the Acre-Safad main road. From here it follows the western boundary of Kafr I'nan village until it reaches the Tiberias-Acre sub-district boundary line, passing to the west of the junction of the Acre-Safad and Lubiya-Kafr I'nan roads. From south-west corner of Kafr I'nan village the boundary line follows the western boundary of the Tiberias sub-district to a point close to the boundary line between the villages of Maghar and Eilabun, thence bulging out to the west to include as much of the eastern part of the plain of Battuf as is necessary for the reservoir proposed by the Jewish Agency for the irrigation of lands to the south and east.

The boundary rejoins the Tiberias sub-district boundary at a point on the Nazareth-Tiberias road south-east of the built-up area of Tur'an; thence it runs southwards, at first following the sub-district boundary and then passing between the Kadoorie Agricultural School and Mount Tabor, to a point due south at the base of Mount Tabor. From here it runs due west, parallel to the horizontal grid line 230, to the north-east corner of the village lands of Tel Adashim. It then runs to the north-west corner of these lands, whence it turns south and west so as to include in the Arab State the sources of the Nazareth water supply in Yafa village. On reaching Ginneiger it follows the eastern, northern and western boundaries of the lands of this village to their south-west corner, whence it proceeds in a straight line to a point on the Haifa-Afula railway on the boundary between the villages of Sarid and El Mujeidil. This is the point of intersection.

The south-western boundary of the area of the Arab State in Galilee takes a line from this point, passing northwards along the eastern boundaries of Sarid and Gevat to the north-eastern corner of Nahalal, proceeding thence across the land of Kefar ha Horesh to a central point on the southern boundary of the village of `Ilut, thence westwards along that village boundary to the eastern boundary of Beit Lahm, thence northwards and north-eastwards along its western boundary to the north-eastern corner of Waldheim and thence north-westwards across the village lands of Shafa 'Amr to the south-eastern corner of Ramat Yohanan'. From here it runs due north-north-east to a point on the Shafa 'Amr-Haifa road, west of its junction with the road to I'Billin. From there it proceeds north-east to a point on the southern boundary of I'Billin situated to the west of the I'Billin-Birwa road. Thence along that boundary to its westernmost point, whence it turns to the north, follows across the village land of Tamra to the north-westernmost corner and along the western boundary of Julis until it reaches the Acre-Safad road. It then runs westwards along the southern side of the Safad-Acre road to the Galilee-Haifa District boundary, from which point it follows that boundary to the sea.

The boundary of the hill country of Samaria and Judea starts on the Jordan River at the Wadi Malih south-east of Beisan and runs due west to meet the Beisan-Jericho road and then follows the western side of that road in a north-westerly direction to the junction of the boundaries of the sub-districts of Beisan, Nablus, and Jenin. From that point it follows the Nablus-Jenin sub-district boundary westwards for a distance of about three kilometres and then turns north-westwards, passing to the east of the built-up areas of the villages of Jalbun and Faqqu'a, to the boundary of the sub-districts of Jenin and Beisan at a point north-east of Nuris. Thence it proceeds first north-westwards to a point due north of the built-up area of Zir'in and then westwards to the Afula-Jenin railway, thence north-westwards along the district boundary line to the point of intersection on the Hejaz railway. From here the boundary runs south-westwards, including the built-up area and some of the land of the village of Kh.Lid in the Arab State to cross the Haifa-Jenin road at a point on the district boundary between Haifa and Samaria west of El Mansi. It follows this boundary to the southernmost point of the village of El Buteimat. From here it follows the northern and eastern boundaries of the village of Ar'ara, rejoining the Haifa-Samaria district boundary at Wadi'Ara, and thence proceeding south-south-westwards in an approximately straight line joining up with the western boundary of Qaqun to a point east of the railway line on the eastern boundary of Qaqun village. From here it runs along the railway line some distance to the east of it to a point just east of the Tulkarm railway station. Thence the boundary follows a line half-way between the railway and the Tulkarm-Qalqiliya-Jaljuliya and Ras el Ein road to a point just east of Ras el Ein station, whence it proceeds along the railway some distance to the east of it to the point on the railway line south of the junction of the Haifa-Lydda and Beit Nabala lines, whence it proceeds along the southern border of Lydda airport to its south-west corner, thence in a south-westerly direction to a point just west of the built-up area of Sarafand el'Amar, whence it turns south, passing just to the west of the built-up area of Abu el Fadil to the north-east corner of the lands of Beer Ya'Aqov. (The boundary line should be so demarcated as to allow direct access from the Arab State to the airport.) Thence the boundary line follows the western and southern boundaries of Ramle village, to the north-east corner of El Na'ana village, thence in a straight line to the southernmost point of El Barriya, along the eastern boundary of that village and the southern boundary of 'Innaba village. Thence it turns north to follow the southern side of the Jaffa-Jerusalem road until El Qubab, whence it follows the road to the boundary of Abu Shusha. It runs along the eastern boundaries of Abu Shusha, Seidun, Hulda to the southernmost point of Hulda, thence westwards in a straight line to the north-eastern corner of Umm Kalkha, thence following the northern boundaries of Umm Kalkha, Qazaza and the northern and western boundaries of Mukhezin to the Gaza District boundary and thence runs across the village lands of El Mismiya, El Kabira, and Yasur to the southern point of intersection, which is midway between the built-up areas of Yasur and Batani Sharqi.

From the southern point of intersection the boundary lines run north-westwards between the villages of Gan Yavne and Barqa to the sea at a point half way between Nabi Yunis and Minat el Qila, and south-eastwards to a point west of Qastina, whence it turns in a south-westerly direction, passing to the east of the built-up areas of Es Sawafir, Es Sharqiya and Ibdis. From the south-east corner of Ibdis village it runs to a point south-west of the built-up area of Beit 'Affa, crossing the Hebron-El Majdal road just to the west of the built-up area of Iraq Suweidan. Thence it proceeds southwards along the western village boundary of El Faluja to the Beersheba sub-district boundary. It then runs across the tribal lands of 'Arab el Jubarat to a point on the boundary between the sub-districts of Beersheba and Hebron north of Kh. Khuweilifa, whence it proceeds in a south-westerly direction to a point on the Beersheba-Gaza main road two kilometres to the north-west of the town. It then turns south-eastwards to reach Wadi Sab' at a point situated one kilometre to the west of it. From here it turns north-eastwards and proceeds along Wadi Sab' and along the Beersheba-Hebron road for a distance of one kilometre, whence it turns eastwards and runs in a straight line to Kh. Kuseifa to join the Beersheba-Hebron sub-district boundary. It then follows the Beersheba-Hebron boundary eastwards to a point north of Ras Ez Zuweira, only departing from it so as to cut across the base of the indentation between vertical grid lines 150 and 160.

About five kilometres north-east of Ras ez Zuweira it turns north, excluding from the Arab State a strip along the coast of the Dead Sea not more than seven kilometres in depth, as far as Ein Geddi, whence it turns due east to join the Transjordan frontier in the Dead Sea.

The northern boundary of the Arab section of the coastal plain runs from a point between Minat el Qila and Nabi Yunis, passing between the built-up areas of Gan Yavne and Barqa to the point of intersection. From here it turns south-westwards, running across the lands of Batani Sharqi, along the eastern boundary of the lands of Beit Daras and across the lands of Julis, leaving the built-up areas of Batani Sharqi and Julis to the westwards, as far as the north-west corner of the lands of Beit Tima. Thence it runs east of El Jiya across the village lands of El Barbara along the eastern boundaries of the villages of Beit Jirja, Deir Suneid and Dimra. From the south-east corner of Dimra the boundary passes across the lands of Beit Hanun, leaving the Jewish lands of Nir-Am to the eastwards. From the south-east corner of Dimra the boundary passes across the lands of Beit Hanun, leaving the Jewish lands of Nir-Am to the eastwards. From the south-east corner of Beit Hanun the line runs south-west to a point south of the parallel grid line 100, then turns north-west for two kilometres, turning again in a south-westerly direction and continuing in an almost straight line to the north-west corner of the village lands of Kirbet Ikhza'a. From there it follows the boundary line of this village to its southernmost point. It then runs in a southernly direction along the vertical grid line 90 to its junction with the horizontal grid line 70. It then turns south-eastwards to Kh. el Ruheiba and then proceeds in a southerly direction to a point known as El Baha, beyond which it crosses the Beersheba-El 'Auja main road to the west of Kh. el Mushrifa. From there it joins Wadi El Zaiyatin just to the west of El Subeita. From there it turns to the north-east and then to the south-east following this Wadi and passes to the east of 'Abda to join Wadi Nafkh. It then bulges to the south-west along Wadi Nafkh. It then bulges to the south-west along Wadi Nafkh, Wadi Ajrim and Wadi Lassan to the point where Wadi Lassan crosses the Egyptian frontier.

The area of the Arab enclave of Jaffa consists of that part of the town-planning area of Jaffa which lies to the west of the Jewish quarters lying south of Tel-Aviv, to the west of the continuation of Herzl street up to its junction with the Jaffa-Jerusalem road, to the south-west of the section of the Jaffa-Jerusalem road lying south-east of that junction, to the west of Miqve Israel lands, to the north-west of Holon local council area, to the north of the line linking up the north-west corner of Holon with the north-east corner of Bat Yam local council area and to the north of Bat Yam local council area. The question of Karton quarter will be decided by the Boundary Commission, bearing in mind among other considerations the desirability of including the smallest possible number of its Arab inhabitants and the largest possible number of its Jewish inhabitants in the Jewish State.

B. THE JEWISH STATE

The north-eastern sector of the Jewish State (Eastern) Galilee) is bounded on the north and west by the Lebanese frontier and on the east by the frontiers of Syria and Transjordan. It includes the whole of the Hula Basin, Lake Tiberias, the whole of the Beisan sub-district, the boundary line being extended to the crest of the Gilboa mountains and the Wadi Malih. From there the Jewish State extends north-west, following the boundary described in respect of the Arab State.

The Jewish Section of the coastal plain extends from a point between Minat et Qila and Nabi Yunis in the Gaza sub-district and includes the towns of Haifa and Tel-Aviv, leaving Jaffa as an enclave of the Arab State. The eastern frontier of the Jewish State follows the boundary described in respect of the Arab State.

The Beersheba area comprises the whole of the Beersheba sub-district, including the Negeb and the eastern part of the Gaza sub-district, but excluding the town of Beersheba and those areas described in respect of the Arab State. It includes also a strip of land along the Dead Sea stretching from the Beersheba-Hebron sub-district boundary line to Ein Geddi, as described in respect of the Arab State.

C. THE CITY OF JERUSALEM

The boundaries of the City of Jerusalem are as defined in the recommendations on the City of Jerusalem. (See Part III, Section B, below).

PART III

City of Jerusalem

A. SPECIAL REGIME

The City of Jerusalem shall be established as a *corpus separatum* under a special international regime and shall be administered by the United Nations. The Trusteeship Council shall be designated to discharge the responsibilities of the Administering Authority on behalf of the United Nations.

B. BOUNDARIES OF THE CITY

The City of Jerusalem shall include the present municipality of Jerusalem plus the surrounding villages and towns, the most eastern of which shall be Abu Dis; the most southern, Bethlehem; the most western, Ein Karim (including also the built-up area of Motsa); and the most northern Shu'fat, as indicated on the attached sketch-map (annex B).

C. STATUTE OF THE CITY

The Trusteeship Council shall, within five months of the approval of the present plan, elaborate and approve a detailed Statute of the City which shall contain inter alia the substance of the following provisions:

1. *Government machinery; special objectives.* The Administering Authority in discharging its administrative obligations shall pursue the following special objectives:

(a) To protect and to preserve the unique spiritual and religious interests located in the city of the three great monotheistic faiths throughout the world, Christian, Jewish and Moslem; to this end to ensure that order and peace, and especially religious peace, reign in Jerusalem;

(b) To foster co-operation among all the inhabitants of the city in their own interests as well as in order to encourage and support the peaceful development of the mutual relations between the two Palestinian peoples throughout the Holy Land; to promote the security, well-being and any constructive measures of development of the residents, having regard to the special circumstances and customs of the various peoples and communities.

2. *Governor and administrative staff.* A Governor of the City of Jerusalem shall be appointed by the Trusteeship Council and shall be responsible to it. He shall be selected on the basis of special qualifications and without regard to nationality. He shall not, however, be a citizen of either State in Palestine.

The Governor shall represent the United Nations in the City and shall exercise on their behalf all powers of administration, including the conduct of external affairs. He shall be assisted by an administrative staff classed as international officers in the meaning of Article 100 of the Charter and chosen whenever practicable from the residents of the city and of the rest of Palestine on a non-discriminatory basis. A detailed plan for the organization of the administration of the city shall be submitted by the Governor to the Trusteeship Council and duly approved by it.

3. *Local autonomy.* (a) The existing local autonomous units in the territory of the city (villages, townships and municipalities) shall enjoy wide powers of local government and administration.

(b) The Governor shall study and submit for the consideration and decision of the Trusteeship Council a plan for the establishment of a special town units consisting respectively, of the Jewish and Arab sections of new Jerusalem. The new town units shall continue to form part of the present municipality of Jerusalem.

4. *Security measures.* (a) The City of Jerusalem shall be demilitarized; its neutrality shall be declared and preserved, and no para-military formations, exercises or activities shall be permitted within its borders.

(b) Should the administration of the City of Jerusalem be seriously obstructed or prevented by the non-co-operation or interference of one or more sections of the population, the Governor shall have authority to take such measures as may be necessary to restore the effective functioning of the administration.

(c) To assist in the maintenance of internal law and order and especially for the protection of the Holy Places and religious buildings and sites in the city, the Governor shall organize a special police force of adequate strength, the members of which shall be recruited outside of Palestine. The Governor shall be empowered to direct such budgetary provision as may be necessary for the maintenance of this force.

5. *Legislative organization.* A Legislative Council, elected by adult residents of the city irrespective of nationality on the basis of universal and secret suffrage and proportional representation, shall have powers of legislation and taxation. No legislative measures shall, however, conflict or interfere with the provisions which will be set forth in the Statute of the City, nor shall any law, regulation, or official action prevail over them. The Statute shall grant to the Governor a right of

vetoing bills inconsistent with the provisions referred to in the preceding sentence. It shall also empower him to promulgate temporary ordinances in case the council fails to adopt in time a bill deemed essential to the normal functioning of the administration.

6. *Administration of justice.* The Statute shall provide for the establishment of an independent judiciary system, including a court of appeal. All the inhabitants of the City shall be subject to it.

7. *Economic union and economic regime.* The City of Jerusalem shall be included in the Economic Union of Palestine and be bound by all stipulations of the undertaking and of any treaties issued therefrom, as well as by the decision of the Joint Economic Board. The headquarters of the Economic Board shall be established in the territory of the City.

The Statute shall provide for the regulation of economic matters not falling within the regime of the Economic Union, on the basis of equal treatment and non-discrimination for all members of the United Nations and their nationals.

8. *Freedom of transit and visit; control of residents.* Subject to considerations of security, and of economic welfare as determined by the Governor under the directions of the Trusteeship Council, freedom of entry into, and residence within, the borders of the City shall be guaranteed for the residents or citizens of the Arab and Jewish States. Immigration into, and residence within, the borders of the city for nationals of other States shall be controlled by the Governor under the directions of the Trusteeship Council.

9. *Relations with the Arab and Jewish States.* Representatives of the Arab and Jewish States shall be accredited to the Governor of the City and charged with the protection of the interests of their States and nationals in connexion with the international administration of the City.

10. *Official languages.* Arabic and Hebrew shall be the official languages of the city. This will not preclude the adoption of one or more additional working languages, as may be required.

11. *Citizenship.* All the residents shall become ipso facto citizens of the City of Jerusalem unless they opt for citizenship of the State of which they have been citizens or, if Arabs or Jews, have filed notice of

intention to become citizens of the Arab or Jewish State respectively, according to part I, section B, paragraph 9, of this plan.

The Trusteeship Council shall make arrangements for consular protection of the citizens of the City outside its territory.

12. *Freedoms of Citizens.* (a) Subject only to the requirements of public order and morals, the inhabitants of the City shall be ensured the enjoyment of human rights and fundamental freedoms, including freedom of conscience, religion and worship, language, education, speech and press, assembly and association, and petition.

(b) No discrimination of any kind shall be made between the inhabitants on the grounds of race, religion, language or sex.

(c) All persons within the City shall be entitled to equal protection of the laws.

(d) The family law and personal status of the various persons and communities and their religious interests, including endowments, shall be respected.

(e) Except as may be required for the maintenance of public order and good government, no measure shall be taken to obstruct or interfere with the enterprise of religious or charitable bodies of all faiths or to discriminate against any representative or member of these bodies on the ground of his religion or nationality.

(f) The City shall ensure adequate primary and secondary education for the Arab and Jewish communities respectively, in their own languages and in accordance with their cultural traditions.

The right of each community to maintain its own schools for the education of its own members in its own language, while conforming to such educational requirements of a general nature as the City may impose, shall not be denied or impaired. Foreign educational establishments shall continue their activity on the basis of their existing rights.

(g) No restriction shall be imposed on the free use by any inhabitant of the City of any language in private intercourse, in commerce, in religion, in the Press or in publications of any kind, or at public meetings.

13. *Holy Places.* (a) Existing rights in respect of Holy Places and religious buildings or sites shall not be denied or impaired.

(b) Free access to the Holy Places and religious buildings or sites and the free exercise of worship shall be secured in conformity with existing rights and subject to the requirements of public order and decorum.

(c) Holy Places and religious buildings or sites shall be preserved. No act shall be permitted which may in any way impair their sacred character. If at any time it appears to the Governor that any particular Holy Place, religious building or site is in need of urgent repair, the Governor may call upon the community or communities concerned to carry out such repair. The Governor may carry it out himself at the expense of the community or communities concerned if no action is taken within a reasonable time.

(d) No taxation shall be levied in respect of any Holy Place, religious building or site which was exempt from taxation on the date of the creation of the City. No change in the incidence of such taxation shall be made which would either discriminate between the owners or occupiers of Holy Places, religious buildings or sites, or would place such owners or occupiers in a position less favourable in relation to the general incidence of taxation than existed at the time of the adoption of the Assembly's recommendations.

14. *Special powers of the Governor in respect of the Holy Places, religious buildings and sites in the City and in any part of Palestine.* (a) The protection of the Holy Places, religious buildings and sites located in the City of Jerusalem shall be a special concern of the Governor.

(b) With relation to such places, buildings and sites in Palestine outside the city, the Governor shall determine, on the ground of powers granted to him by the Constitutions of both States, whether the provisions of the Constitutions of the Arab and Jewish States in Palestine dealing therewith and the religious rights appertaining thereto are being properly applied and respected.

(c) The Governor shall also be empowered to make decisions on the basis of existing rights in cases of disputes which may arise between the different religious communities or the rites of a religious community in respect of the Holy Places, religious buildings and sites in any part of Palestine.

In this task he may be assisted by a consultative council of representatives of different denominations acting in an advisory capacity.

D. DURATION OF THE
SPECIAL REGIME

The Statute elaborated by the Trusteeship Council on the aforementioned principles shall come into force not later than 1 October 1948. It shall remain in force in the first instance for a period of ten years, unless the Trusteeship Council finds it necessary to undertake a re-examination of these provisions at an earlier date. After the expiration of this period the whole scheme shall be subject to re-examination by the Trusteeship Council in the light of the experience acquired with its functioning. The residents of the City shall be then free to express by means of a referendum their wishes as to possible modifications of the regime of the City.

PART IV

CAPITULATIONS

States whose nationals have in the past enjoyed in Palestine the privileges and immunities of foreigners, including the benefits of consular jurisdiction and protection, as formerly enjoyed by capitulation or usage in the Ottoman Empire, are invited to renounce any right pertaining to them to the re-establishment of such privileges and immunities in the proposed Arab and Jewish States and the City of Jerusalem.

* * *

Notes

1/ See Official Records of the second session of the General Assembly, Supplement No. 11, Volumes I-IV.

2/ This resolution was adopted without reference to a Committee.

3/ The following stipulation shall be added to the declaration concerning the Jewish State: "In the Jewish State adequate facilities shall be given to Arab-speaking citizens for the use of their language, either orally or in writing, in the legislature, before the Courts and in the administration."

4/ In the declaration concerning the Arab State, the words "by an Arab in the Jewish State" should be replaced by the words "by a Jew in the Arab State".

5/ The boundary lines described in part II are indicated in Annex A. The base map used in marking and describing this boundary is "Palestine 1:250000" published by the Survey of Palestine, 1946.

Annex A

Plan of Partition with Economic Union
Annex B

City of Jerusalem
Boundaries Proposed By The Ad Hoc Committee On The Palestinian Question

Appendix D

United Nations General Assembly Resolution 194 (III), December 1948

194 (III). PALESTINE — PROGRESS REPORT OF THE UNITED NATIONS MEDIATOR

The General Assembly,

Having considered further the situation in Palestine,

1. *Expresses* its deep appreciation of the progress achieved through the good offices of the late United Nations Mediator in promoting a peaceful adjustment of the future situation of Palestine, for which cause he sacrificed his life; and

Extends its thanks to the Acting Mediator and his staff for their continued efforts and devotion to duty in Palestine;

2. *Establishes* a Conciliation Commission consisting of three States members of the United Nations which shall have the following functions:

(a) To assume, in so far as it considers necessary in existing circumstances, the functions given to the United Nations Mediator on Palestine by resolution 186 (S-2) of the General Assembly of 14 May 1948;

(b) To carry out the specific functions and directives given to it by the present resolution and such additional functions and directives as may be given to it by the General Assembly or by the Security Council;

(c) To undertake, upon the request of the Security Council, any of the functions now assigned to the United Nations Mediator on Palestine or to the United Nations Truce Commission by resolutions of the Security

Council; upon such request to the Conciliation Commission by the Security Council with respect to all the remaining functions of the United Nations Mediator on Palestine under Security Council resolutions, the office of the Mediator shall be terminated;

3. *Decides* that a Committee of the Assembly, consisting of China, France, the Union of Soviet Socialist Republics, the United Kingdom and the United States of America, shall present, before the end of the first part of the present session of the General Assembly, for the approval of the Assembly, a proposal concerning the names of the three States which will constitute the Conciliation Commission;

4. *Requests* the Commission to begin its functions at once, with a view to the establishment of contact between the parties themselves and the Commission at the earliest possible date;

5. *Calls upon* the Governments and authorities concerned to extend the scope of the negotiations provided for in the Security Council's resolution of 16 November 1948 and to seek agreement by negotiations conducted either with the Conciliation Commission or directly, with a view to the final settlement of all questions outstanding between them;

6. *Instructs* the Conciliation Commission to take steps to assist the Governments and authorities concerned to achieve a final settlement of all questions outstanding between them;

7. *Resolves* that the Holy Places—including Nazareth—religious buildings and sites in Palestine should be protected and free access to them assured, in accordance with existing rights and historical practice; that arrangements to this end should be under effective United Nations supervision; that the United Nations Conciliation Commission, in presenting to the fourth regular session of the General Assembly its detailed proposals for a permanent international regime for the territory of Jerusalem, should include recommendations concerning the Holy Places in that territory; that with regard to the Holy Places in the rest of Palestine the Commission should call upon the political authorities of the areas concerned to give appropriate formal guarantees as to the protection of the Holy Places and access to them; and that these undertakings should be presented to the General Assembly for approval;

8. *Resolves* that, in view of its association with three world religions, the Jerusalem area, including the present municipality of Jerusalem plus the surrounding villages and towns, the most eastern of which shall be Abu Dis; the most southern, Bethlehem; the most western, Ein Karim (including also the built-up area of Motsa); and the most northern, Shu'fat, should be accorded special and separate treatment from the rest of Palestine and should be placed under effective United Nations control;

Requests the Security Council to take further steps to ensure the demilitarization of Jerusalem at the earliest possible date;

Instructs the Conciliation Commission to present to the fourth regular session of the General Assembly detailed proposals for a permanent international regime for the Jerusalem area which will provide for the maximum local autonomy for distinctive groups consistent with the special international status of the Jerusalem area;

The Conciliation Commission is authorized to appoint a United Nations representative, who shall co-operate with the local authorities with respect to the interim administration of the Jerusalem area;

9. *Resolves* that, pending agreement on more detailed arrangements among the Governments and authorities concerned, the freest possible access to Jerusalem by road, rail or air should be accorded to all inhabitants of Palestine;

Instructs the Conciliation Commission to report immediately to the Security Council, for appropriate action by that organ, any attempt by any party to impede such access;

10. *Instructs* the Conciliation Commission to seek arrangements among the Governments and authorities concerned which will facilitate the economic development of the area, including arrangements for access to ports and airfields and the use of transportation and communication facilities;

11. *Resolves* that the refugees wishing to return to their homes and live at peace with their neighbours should be permitted to do so at the earliest practicable date, and that compensation should be paid for the property of those choosing not to return and for loss of or damage to property which, under principles of international law or in equity,

should be made good by the Governments or authorities responsible; Instructs the Conciliation Commission to facilitate the repatriation, resettlement and economic and social rehabilitation of the refugees and the payment of compensation, and to maintain close relations with the Director of the United Nations Relief for Palestine Refugees and, through him, with the appropriate organs and agencies of the United Nations;

12. *Authorizes* the Conciliation Commission to appoint such subsidiary bodies and to employ such technical experts, acting under its authority, as it may find necessary for the effective discharge of its functions and responsibilities under the present resolution;

The Conciliation Commission will have its official headquarters at Jerusalem. The authorities responsible for maintaining order in Jerusalem will be responsible for taking all measures necessary to ensure the security of the Commission. The Secretary-General will provide a limited number of guards to the protection of the staff and premises of the Commission;

13. *Instructs* the Conciliation Commission to render progress reports periodically to the Secretary-General for transmission to the Security Council and to the Members of the United Nations;

14. *Calls upon* all Governments and authorities concerned to co-operate with the Conciliation Commission and to take all possible steps to assist in the implementation of the present resolution;

15. *Requests* the Secretary-General to provide the necessary staff and facilities and to make appropriate arrangements to provide the necessary funds required in carrying out the terms of the present resolution.

* * *

At the 186th plenary meeting on 11 December 1948, a committee of the Assembly consisting of the five States designated in paragraph 3 of the above resolution proposed that the following three States should constitute the Conciliation Commission:

France, Turkey, United States of America.

The proposal of the Committee having been adopted by the General Assembly at the same meeting, the Conciliation Commission is therefore composed of the above-mentioned three States.

Appendix E

Palestinian National Charter, 1964

(Al-Mithaq Al-Kawmee Al-Philisteeni)*

INTRODUCTION

We, the Palestinian Arab people, who waged fierce and continuous battles to safeguard its homeland, to defend its dignity and honor, and who offered all through the years continuous caravans of immortal martyrs, and who wrote the noblest pages of sacrifice, offering and giving.

We, the Palestinian Arab people, who faced the forces of evil, injustice and aggression, against whom the forces of international Zionism and colonialism conspire and worked to displace it, dispossess it from its homeland and property, abused what is holy in it and who in spite of all this refused to weaken or submit.

We, the Palestinian Arab people, who believe in its Arabism and in its right to regain its homeland, to realize its freedom and dignity, and who have determined to amass its forces and mobilize its efforts and capabilities in order to continue its struggle and to move forward on the path of holy war (al-jihad) until complete and final victory has been attained.

We, the Palestinian Arab people, based on our right of self-defense and the complete restoration of our lost homeland- a right that has been recognized by international covenants and common practices including the Charter of the United Nations-and in implementation of the principles of human rights, and comprehending the international political relations, with its various ramifications and dimensions, and considering the past experiences in all that pertains to the causes of the catastrophe, and the means to face it,

And embarking from the Palestinian Arab reality, and for the sake of the honor of the Palestinian individual and his right to free and dignified life,

And realizing the national grave responsibility placed upon our shoulders, for the sake of all this,

We, the Palestinian Arab people, dictate and declare this Palestinian National Charter and swear to realize it.

Article 1. Palestine is an Arab homeland bound by strong Arab national ties to the rest of the Arab Countries and which together form the great Arab homeland.

Article 2: Palestine, with its boundaries at the time of the British Mandate, is a indivisible territorial unit.

Article 3: The Palestinian Arab people has the legitimate right to its homeland and isan inseparable part of the Arab Nation. It shares the sufferings and aspirations of the Arab Nation and its struggle for freedom, sovereignty, progress and unity.

Article 4: The people of Palestine determine its destiny when it completes the liberation of its homeland in accordance with its own wishes and free will and choice.

Article 5: The Palestinian personality is a permanent and genuine characteristic that does not disappear. It is transferred from fathers to sons.

Article 6: The Palestinians are those Arab citizens who were living normally in Palestine up to 1947, whether they remained or were expelled. Every child who was born to a Palestinian Arab father after this date, whether in Palestine or outside, is a Palestinian.

Article 7: Jews of Palestinian origin are considered Palestinians if they are willing to live peacefully and loyally in Palestine.

Article 8: Bringing up Palestinian youth in an Arab and nationalist manner is a fundamental national duty. All means of guidance, education and enlightenment should be utilized to introduce the youth to its homeland in a deep spiritual way that will constantly and firmly bind them together.

Article 9: Ideological doctrines, whether political, social, or economic, shall not distract the people of Palestine from the primary duty of liberating their homeland. All Palestinian constitute one national front and work with all their feelings and material potentialities to free their homeland.

Article 10: Palestinians have three mottos: National Unity, National Mobilization, and Liberation. Once liberation is completed, the people of Palestine shall choose for its public life whatever political, economic, or social system they want.

Article 11: The Palestinian people firmly believe in Arab unity, and in order to play its role in realizing this goal, it must, at this stage of its struggle, preserve its Palestinian personality and all its constituents. It must strengthen the consciousness of its existence and stance and stand against any attempt or plan that may weaken or disintegrate its personality.

Article 12: Arab unity and the liberation of Palestine are two complementary goals; each prepares for the attainment of the other. Arab unity leads to the liberation of Palestine, and the liberation of Palestine leads to Arab unity. Working for both must go side by side.

Article 13: The destiny of the Arab Nation and even the essence of Arab existence are firmly tied to the destiny of the Palestine question. From this firm bond stems the effort and struggle of the Arab Nation to liberate Palestine. The people of Palestine assume a vanguard role in achieving this sacred national goal.

Article 14: The liberation of Palestine, from an Arab viewpoint, is a national duty. Its responsibilities fall upon the entire Arab nation, governments and peoples, the Palestinian peoples being in the forefront. For this purpose, the Arab nation must mobilize its military, spiritual and material potentialities; specifically, it must give to the Palestinian Arab people all possible support and backing and place at its disposal all opportunities and means to enable them to perform their role in liberating their homeland.

Article 15: The liberation of Palestine, from a spiritual viewpoint, prepares for the Holy Land an atmosphere of tranquillity and peace, in which all the Holy Places will be safeguarded, and the freedom to worship and to visit will be guaranteed for all, without any discrimination of race, color, language, or religion. For all this, the

Palestinian people look forward to the support of all the spiritual forces in the world.

Article 16: The liberation of Palestine, from an international viewpoint, is a defensive act necessitated by the demands of self-defense as stated in the Charter of the United Nations. For that, the people of Palestine, desiring to befriend all nations which love freedom, justice, and peace, look forward to their support in restoring the legitimate situation to Palestine, establishing peace and security in its territory, and enabling its people to exercise national sovereignty and freedom.

Article 17: The partitioning of Palestine, which took place in 1947, and the establishment of Israel are illegal and null and void, regardless of the loss of time, because they were contrary to the will of the Palestinian people and its natural right to its homeland, and were in violation of the basic principles embodied in the Charter of the United Nations, foremost among which is the right to self-determination.

Article 18: The Balfour Declaration, the Palestine Mandate System, and all that has been based on them are considered null and void. The claims of historic and spiritual ties between Jews and Palestine are not in agreement with the facts of history or with the true basis of sound statehood. Judaism, because it is a divine religion, is not a nationality with independent existence. Furthermore, the Jews are not one people with an independent personality because they are citizens to their states.

Article 19: Zionism is a colonialist movement in its inception, aggressive and expansionist in its goal, racist in its configurations, and fascist in its means and aims. Israel, in its capacity as the spearhead of this destructive movement and as the pillar of colonialism, is a permanent source of tension and turmoil in the Middle East, in particular, and to the international community in general. Because of this, the people of Palestine are worthy of the support and sustenance of the community of nations.

Article 20: The causes of peace and security and the requirements of right and justice demand from all nations, in order to safeguard true relationships among peoples and to maintain the loyalty of citizens to their homeland, that they consider Zionism an illegal movement and outlaw its presence and activities.

Article 21: The Palestinian people believes in the principles of justice, freedom, sovereignty, self-determination, human dignity, and the right of peoples to practice these principles. It also supports all international efforts to bring about peace on the basis of justice and free international cooperation.

Article 22: The Palestinian people believe in peaceful co-existence on the basis of legal existence, for there can be no coexistence with aggression, nor can there be peace with occupation and colonialism.

Article 23: In realizing the goals and principles of this Covenant, the Palestine Liberation Organization carries out its full role to liberate Palestine in accordance with the basic law of this Organization.

Article 24: This Organization does not exercise any territorial sovereignty over the West Bank in the Hashemite Kingdom of Jordan, on the Gaza Strip or in the Himmah Area. Its activities will be on the national popular level in the liberational, organizational, political and financial fields.

Article 25: This Organization is in charge of the movement of the Palestinian people in its struggle to liberate its homeland in all liberational, organizational, and financial matters, and in all other needs of the Palestine Question in the Arab and international spheres.

Article 26: The Liberation Organization cooperates with all Arab governments, each according to its ability, and does not interfere in the internal affairs of any Arab states.

Article 27: This Organization shall have its flag, oath and a national anthem. All this shall be resolved in accordance with special regulations.

Article 28: The basic law for the Palestine Liberation Organization is attached to this Charter. This law defines the manner of establishing the Organization, its organs, institutions, the specialties of each one of them, and all the needed duties thrust upon it in accordance with this Charter.

Article 29: This Charter cannot be amended except by two-thirds majority of the members of the National Council of the Palestine Liberation Organization in a special session called for this purpose.

*Adopted in 1964 by the 1st Palestinian Conference

* "Al-Kawmee" has no exact equivalent in English but reflects the notion of Pan-Arabism.

Appendix F

Resolution of Arab League, Khartoum, September 1967

1. The conference has affirmed the unity of Arab ranks, the unity of joint action and the need for coordination and for the elimination of all differences. The Kings, Presidents and representatives of the other Arab Heads of State at the conference have affirmed their countries' stand by and implementation of the Arab Solidarity Charter which was signed at the third Arab summit conference in Casablanca.

2. The conference has agreed on the need to consolidate all efforts to eliminate the effects of the aggression on the basis that the occupied lands are Arab lands and that the burden of regaining these lands falls on all the Arab States.

3. The Arab Heads of State have agreed to unite their political efforts at the international and diplomatic level to eliminate the effects of the aggression and to ensure the withdrawal of the aggressive Israeli forces from the Arab lands which have been occupied since the aggression of June 5. This will be done within the framework of the main principles by which the Arab States abide, namely, no peace with Israel, no recognition of Israel, no negotiations with it, and insistence on the rights of the Palestinian people in their own country.

4. The conference of Arab Ministers of Finance, Economy and Oil recommended that suspension of oil pumping be used as a weapon in the battle. However, after thoroughly studying the matter, the summit conference has come to the conclusion that the oil pumping can itself be used as a positive weapon, since oil is an Arab resource which can be used to strengthen the economy of the Arab States directly affected by the aggression, so that these States will be able to stand firm in the battle. The conference has, therefore, decided to resume the pumping of oil, since oil is a positive Arab resource that can be used in the service of Arab goals. It can contribute to the efforts to enable those

Arab States which were exposed to the aggression and thereby lost economic resources to stand firm and eliminate the effects of the aggression. The oil-producing States have, in fact, participated in the efforts to enable the States affected by the aggression to stand firm in the face of any economic pressure.

5. The participants in the conference have approved the plan proposed by Kuwait to set up an Arab Economic and Social Development Fund on the basis of the recommendation of the Baghdad conference of Arab Ministers of Finance, Economy and Oil.

6. The participants have agreed on the need to adopt the necessary measures to strengthen military preparation to face all eventualities. The conference has decided to expedite the elimination of foreign bases in the Arab States

Appendix G

United Nations Security Council Resolution 242, November 1967

The Security Council,

Expressing its continuing concern with the grave situation in the Middle East,

Emphasizing the inadmissibility of the acquisition of territory by war and the need to work for a just and lasting peace in which every State in the area can live in security,

Emphasizing further that all Member States in their acceptance of the Charter of the United Nations have undertaken a commitment to act in accordance with Article 2 of the Charter,

1. *Affirms* that the fulfilment of Charter principles requires the establishment of a just and lasting peace in the Middle East which should include the application of both the following principles:

(i) Withdrawal of Israel armed forces from territories occupied in the recent conflict;

(ii) Termination of all claims or states of belligerency and respect for and acknowledgment of the sovereignty, territorial integrity and political independence of every State in the area and their right to live in peace within secure and recognized boundaries free from threats or acts of force;

2. *Affirms further* the necessity

(a) For guaranteeing freedom of navigation through international waterways in the area;

(b) For achieving a just settlement of the refugee problem;

(c) For guaranteeing the territorial inviolability and political independence of every State in the area, through measures including the establishment of demilitarized zones;

3. *Requests* the Secretary-General to designate a Special Representative to proceed to the Middle East to establish and maintain contacts with the States concerned in order to promote agreement and assist efforts to achieve a peaceful and accepted settlement in accordance with the provisions and principles in this resolution;

4. *Requests* the Secretary-General to report to the Security Council on the progress of the efforts of the Special Representative as soon as possible.

Adopted unanimously at the 1382nd meeting.

Appendix H

PLO Charter, July 1968

Article 1: Palestine is the homeland of the Arab Palestinian people; it is an indivisible part of the Arab homeland, and the Palestinian people are an integral part of the Arab nation.

Article 2: Palestine, with the boundaries it had during the British Mandate, is an indivisible territorial unit.

Article 3: The Palestinian Arab people possess the legal right to their homeland and have the right to determine their destiny after achieving the liberation of their country in accordance with their wishes and entirely of their own accord and will.

Article 4: The Palestinian identity is a genuine, essential, and inherent characteristic; it is transmitted from parents to children. The Zionist occupation and the dispersal of the Palestinian Arab people, through the disasters which befell them, do not make them lose their Palestinian identity and their membership in the Palestinian community, nor do they negate them.

Article 5: The Palestinians are those Arab nationals who, until 1947, normally resided in Palestine regardless of whether they were evicted from it or have stayed there. Anyone born, after that date, of a Palestinian father - whether inside Palestine or outside it - is also a Palestinian.

Article 6: The Jews who had normally resided in Palestine until the beginning of the Zionist invasion will be considered Palestinians.

Article 7: That there is a Palestinian community and that it has material, spiritual, and historical connection with Palestine are indisputable facts. It is a national duty to bring up individual Palestinians in an Arab revolutionary manner. All means of information and education must be adopted in order to acquaint the Palestinian with his country in the most profound manner, both spiritual and material, that is possible. He must be prepared for the armed struggle and ready to sacrifice his wealth and his life in order to win back his homeland and bring about its liberation.

Article 8: The phase in their history, through which the Palestinian people are now living, is that of national (watani) struggle for the liberation of Palestine. Thus the conflicts among the Palestinian national forces are secondary, and should be ended for the sake of the basic conflict that exists between the forces of Zionism and of imperialism on the one hand, and the Palestinian Arab people on the other. On this basis the Palestinian masses, regardless of whether they are residing in the national homeland or in diaspora (mahajir) constitute - both their organizations and the individuals - one national front working for the retrieval of Palestine and its liberation through armed struggle.

Article 9: Armed struggle is the only way to liberate Palestine. Thus it is the overall strategy, not merely a tactical phase. The Palestinian Arab people assert their absolute determination and firm resolution to continue their armed struggle and to work for an armed popular revolution for the liberation of their country and their return to it. They also assert their right to normal life in Palestine and to exercise their right to self-determination and sovereignty over it.

Article 10: Commando action constitutes the nucleus of the Palestinian popular liberation war. This requires its escalation, comprehensiveness, and the mobilization of all the Palestinian popular and educational efforts and their organization and involvement in the armed Palestinian revolution. It also requires the achieving of unity for the national (watani) struggle among the different groupings of the Palestinian people, and between the Palestinian people and the Arab masses, so as to secure the continuation of the revolution, its escalation, and victory.

Article 11: The Palestinians will have three mottoes: national (wataniyya) unity, national (qawmiyya) mobilization, and liberation.

Article 12: The Palestinian people believe in Arab unity. In order to contribute their share toward the attainment of that objective, however, they must, at the present stage of their struggle, safeguard their Palestinian identity and develop their consciousness of that identity, and oppose any plan that may dissolve or impair it.

Article 13: Arab unity and the liberation of Palestine are two complementary objectives, the attainment of either of which facilitates the attainment of the other. Thus, Arab unity leads to the liberation of Palestine, the liberation of Palestine leads to Arab unity; and work toward the realization of one objective proceeds side by side with work toward the realization of the other.

Article 14: The destiny of the Arab nation, and indeed Arab existence itself, depend upon the destiny of the Palestine cause. From this interdependence springs the Arab nation's pursuit of, and striving for, the liberation of Palestine. The people of Palestine play the role of the vanguard in the realization of this sacred *(qawmi)* goal.

Article 15: The liberation of Palestine, from an Arab viewpoint, is a national *(qawmi)* duty and it attempts to repel the Zionist and imperialist aggression against the Arab homeland, and aims at the elimination of Zionism in Palestine. Absolute responsibility for this falls upon the Arab nation - peoples and governments - with the Arab people of Palestine in the vanguard. Accordingly, the Arab nation must mobilize all its military, human, moral, and spiritual capabilities to participate actively with the Palestinian people in the liberation of Palestine. It must, particularly in the phase of the armed Palestinian revolution, offer and furnish the Palestinian people with all possible help, and material and human support, and make available to them the means and opportunities that will enable them to continue to carry out their leading role in the armed revolution, until they liberate their homeland.

Article 16: The liberation of Palestine, from a spiritual point of view, will provide the Holy Land with an atmosphere of safety and tranquility, which in turn will safeguard the country's religious sanctuaries and guarantee freedom of worship and of visit to all, without discrimination of race, color, language, or religion. Accordingly, the people of Palestine look to all spiritual forces in the world for support.

Article 17: The liberation of Palestine, from a human point of view, will restore to the Palestinian individual his dignity, pride, and freedom. Accordingly the Palestinian Arab people look forward to the support of all those who believe in the dignity of man and his freedom in the world.

Article 18: The liberation of Palestine, from an international point of view, is a defensive action necessitated by the demands of self-defense. Accordingly the Palestinian people, desirous as they are of the friendship of all people, look to freedom-loving, and peace-loving states for support in order to restore their legitimate rights in Palestine, to re-establish peace and security in the country, and to enable its people to exercise national sovereignty and freedom.

Article 19: The partition of Palestine in 1947 and the establishment of the state of Israel are entirely illegal, regardless of the passage of time, because they were contrary to the will of the Palestinian people and to their natural right in their homeland, and inconsistent with the principles embodied in the Charter of the United Nations, particularly the right to self-determination.

Article 20: The Balfour Declaration, the Mandate for Palestine, and everything that has been based upon them, are deemed null and void. Claims of historical or religious ties of Jews with Palestine are incompatible with the facts of history and the true conception of what constitutes statehood. Judaism, being a religion, is not an independent nationality. Nor do Jews constitute a single nation with an identity of its own; they are citizens of the states to which they belong.

Article 21: The Arab Palestinian people, expressing themselves by the armed Palestinian revolution, reject all solutions which are substitutes for the total liberation of Palestine and reject all proposals aiming at the liquidation of the Palestinian problem, or its internationalization.

Article 22: Zionism is a political movement organically associated with international imperialism and antagonistic to all action for liberation and to progressive movements in the world. It is racist and fanatic in its nature, aggressive, expansionist, and colonial in its aims, and fascist in its methods. Israel is the instrument of the Zionist movement, and geographical base for world imperialism placed strategically in the midst of the Arab homeland to combat the hopes of the Arab nation for liberation, unity, and progress. Israel is a constant source of threat vis-a-vis peace in the Middle East and the whole world. Since the liberation of Palestine will destroy the Zionist and imperialist presence and will contribute to the establishment of peace in the Middle East, the Palestinian people look for the support of all the progressive and peaceful forces and urge them all, irrespective of their affiliations and beliefs, to offer the Palestinian people all aid and support in their just struggle for the liberation of their homeland.

Article 23: The demand of security and peace, as well as the demand of right and justice, require all states to consider Zionism an illegitimate movement, to outlaw its existence, and to ban its operations, in order that friendly relations among peoples may be preserved, and the loyalty of citizens to their respective homelands safeguarded.

Article 24: The Palestinian people believe in the principles of justice, freedom, sovereignty, self-determination, human dignity, and in the right of all peoples to exercise them.

Article 25: For the realization of the goals of this Charter and its principles, the Palestine Liberation Organization will perform its role in the liberation of Palestine in accordance with the Constitution of this Organization.

Article 26: The Palestine Liberation Organization, representative of the Palestinian revolutionary forces, is responsible for the Palestinian Arab people's movement in its struggle - to retrieve its homeland, liberate and return to it and exercise the right to self-determination in it - in all military, political, and financial fields and also for whatever may be required by the Palestine case on the inter-Arab and international levels.

Article 27: The Palestine Liberation Organization shall cooperate with all Arab states, each according to its potentialities; and will adopt a neutral policy among them in the light of the requirements of the war of liberation; and on this basis it shall not interfere in the internal affairs of any Arab state.

Article 28: The Palestinian Arab people assert the genuineness and independence of their national *(wataniyya)* revolution and reject all forms of intervention, trusteeship, and subordination.

Article 29: The Palestinian people possess the fundamental and genuine legal right to liberate and retrieve their homeland. The Palestinian people determine their attitude toward all states and forces on the basis of the stands they adopt vis-a-vis to the Palestinian revolution to fulfill the aims of the Palestinian people.

Article 30: Fighters and carriers of arms in the war of liberation are the nucleus of the popular army which will be the protective force for the gains of the Palestinian Arab people.

Article 31: The Organization shall have a flag, an oath of allegiance, and an anthem. All this shall be decided upon in accordance with a special regulation.

Article 32: Regulations, which shall be known as the Constitution of the Palestinian Liberation Organization, shall be annexed to this Charter. It will lay down the manner in which the Organization, and its organs and institutions, shall be constituted; the respective competence of each; and the requirements of its obligation under the Charter.

Article 33: This Charter shall not be amended save by [vote of] a majority of two-thirds of the total membership of the National Congress of the Palestine Liberation Organization [taken] at a special session convened for that purpose.

Appendix I

United Nations Security Council Resolution 338, October 1973

The Security Council

1. *Calls upon* all parties to the present fighting to cease all firing and terminate all military activity immediately, no later than 12 hours after the moment of the adoption of this decision, in the positions they now occupy;

2. *Calls upon* the parties concerned to start immediately after the cease-fire the implementation of Security Council resolution 242 (1967) in all of its parts;

3. *Decides that,* immediately and concurrently with the cease-fire, negotiations shall start between the parties concerned under appropriate auspices aimed at establishing a just and durable peace in the Middle East.

Adopted at the 1747th meeting by 14 votes to none [1]

[1] One member (China) did not participate in the voting.

Appendix J

Declaration of Principles, October 1993

<u>Letter dated 8 October 1993 from the Permanent Representatives of the Russian Federation and the United States of America to the United Nations addressed to the Secretary-General</u>

As co-sponsors of the peace process launched at Madrid in October 1991 and witnesses to the signing at Washington, D.C., on 13 September 1993 of the Declaration of Principles on Interim Self-Government Arrangements, including its Annexes, and its Agreed Minutes, by the Government of the State of Israel and the Palestine Liberation Organization, we have the honour to enclose the above document (see annex).

We would be grateful if you would have the present letter and its attachment circulated as an official document of the forty-eighth session of the General Assembly, under agenda item 10, and of the Security Council.

(Signed) Madeleine K. ALBRIGHT Ambassador
Permanent Representative
to the United Nations of the
United States of America

Signed) Yuliy M. VORONTSOV
Ambassador
Permanent Representative
to the United Nations of
the Russian Federation

93-54838 (E) 121093

Letter dated 8 October 1993 from the Permanent
Representative of Israel to the United Nations
addressed to the Secretary-General

I have the honour to enclose the Declaration of Principles on Interim
Self-Government Arrangements, including its Annexes, and its Agreed
Minutes, signed at Washington, D.C., on 13 September 1993 by the
Government of the State of Israel and the Palestine Liberation
Organization and witnessed by the United States of America and the
Russian Federation (see annex).

I would be grateful if you would have the present letter and its
attachment circulated as an official document of the forty-eighth
session of the General Assembly, under agenda item 10, and of the
Security Council.

(Signed) Gad YAACOBI
Ambassador
Permanent Representative

Letter dated 8 October 1993 from the Permanent
Observer of Palestine to the United Nations
addressed to the Secretary-General

I have the honour to enclose the Declaration of Principles on Interim
Self-Government Arrangements, including its Annexes, and its Agreed
Minutes, signed at Washington, D.C., on 13 September 1993 by the
Government of the State of Israel and the Palestine Liberation
Organization and witnessed by the United States of America and the
Russian Federation (see annex).

I would be grateful if you would have the present letter and its
attachment circulated as an official document of the forty-eighth
session of the General Assembly, under agenda item 10, and of the
Security Council.

(Signed) Dr. Nasser AL-KIDWA
Permanent Observer of Palestine
to the United Nations

ANNEX

Declaration of Principles on Interim
Self-Government Arrangements

The Government of the State of Israel and the PLO team (in the Jordanian-Palestinian delegation to the Middle East Peace Conference) (the "Palestinian Delegation"), representing the Palestinian people, agree that it is time to put an end to decades of confrontation and conflict, recognize their mutual legitimate and political rights, and strive to live in peaceful coexistence and mutual dignity and security and achieve a just, lasting and comprehensive peace settlement and historic reconciliation through the agreed political process. Accordingly, the two sides agree to the following principles:

Article I

AIM OF THE NEGOTIATIONS

The aim of the Israeli-Palestinian negotiations within the current Middle East peace process is, among other things, to establish a Palestinian Interim Self-Government Authority, the elected Council (the "Council"), for the Palestinian people in the West Bank and the Gaza Strip, for a transitional period not exceeding five years, leading to a permanent settlement based on Security Council resolutions 242 (1967) and 338 (1973). It is understood that the interim arrangements are an integral part of the whole peace process and that the negotiations on the permanent status will lead to the implementation of Security Council resolutions 242 (1967) and 338 (1973).

Article II

FRAMEWORK FOR THE INTERIM PERIOD

The agreed framework for the interim period is set forth in this Declaration of Principles.

Article III

ELECTIONS

1. In order that the Palestinian people in the West Bank and Gaza Strip may govern themselves according to democratic principles, direct, free and general political elections will be held for the Council under agreed supervision and international observation, while the Palestinian police will ensure public order.

2. An agreement will be concluded on the exact mode and conditions of the elections in accordance with the protocol attached as Annex I, with the goal of holding the elections not later than nine months after the entry into force of this Declaration of Principles.

3. These elections will constitute a significant interim preparatory step toward the realization of the legitimate rights of the Palestinian people and their just requirements.

Article IV

JURISDICTION

Jurisdiction of the Council will cover West Bank and Gaza Strip territory, except for issues that will be negotiated in the permanent status negotiations. The two sides view the West Bank and the Gaza Strip as a single territorial unit, whose integrity will be preserved during the interim period.

Article V

TRANSITIONAL PERIOD AND PERMANENT STATUS NEGOTIATIONS

1. The five-year transitional period will begin upon the withdrawal from the Gaza Strip and Jericho area.

2. Permanent status negotiations will commence as soon as possible, but not later than the beginning of the third year of the interim period, between the Government of Israel and the Palestinian people's representatives.

3. It is understood that these negotiations shall cover remaining issues, including: Jerusalem, refugees, settlements, security arrangements, borders, relations and cooperation with other neighbours, and other issues of common interest.

4. The two parties agree that the outcome of the permanent status negotiations should not be prejudiced or preempted by agreements reached for the interim period.

Article VI

PREPARATORY TRANSFER OF POWERS AND RESPONSIBILITIES

1. Upon the entry into force of this Declaration of Principles and the withdrawal from the Gaza Strip and the Jericho area, a transfer of authority from the Israeli military government and its Civil Administration to the authorized Palestinians for this task, as detailed herein, will commence. This transfer of authority will be of a preparatory nature until the inauguration of the Council.

2. Immediately after the entry into force of this Declaration of Principles and the withdrawal from the Gaza Strip and Jericho area, with the view to promoting economic development in the West Bank and Gaza Strip, authority will be transferred to the Palestinians in the following spheres: education and culture, health, social welfare, direct taxation and tourism. The Palestinian side will commence in building the Palestinian police force, as agreed upon. Pending the inauguration of the Council, the two parties may negotiate the transfer of additional powers and responsibilities, as agreed upon.

Article VII

INTERIM AGREEMENT

1. The Israeli and Palestinian delegations will negotiate an agreement on the interim period (the "Interim Agreement").

2. The Interim Agreement shall specify, among other things, the structure of the Council, the number of its members, and the transfer of powers and responsibilities from the Israeli military government and its Civil Administration to the Council. The Interim Agreement shall also specify the Council's executive authority, legislative authority in accordance with Article IX below, and the independent Palestinian judicial organs.

3. The Interim Agreement shall include arrangements, to be implemented upon the inauguration of the Council, for the assumption by the Council of all of the powers and responsibilities transferred previously in accordance with Article VI above.

4. In order to enable the Council to promote economic growth, upon its inauguration, the Council will establish, among other things, a Palestinian Electricity Authority, a Gaza Sea Port Authority, a Palestinian Development Bank, a Palestinian Export Promotion Board, a Palestinian Environmental Authority, a Palestinian Land Authority and a Palestinian Water Administration Authority and any other Authorities agreed upon, in accordance with the Interim Agreement, that will specify their powers and responsibilities.

5. After the inauguration of the Council, the Civil Administration will be dissolved, and the Israeli military government will be withdrawn.

Article VIII

PUBLIC ORDER AND SECURITY

In order to guarantee public order and internal security for the Palestinians of the West Bank and the Gaza Strip, the Council will establish a strong police force, while Israel will continue to carry the responsibility for defending against external threats, as well as the responsibility for overall security of Israelis for the purpose of safeguarding their internal security and public order.

Article IX

LAWS AND MILITARY ORDERS

1. The Council will be empowered to legislate, in accordance with the Interim Agreement, within all authorities transferred to it.

2. Both parties will review jointly laws and military orders presently in force in remaining spheres.

Article X

JOINT ISRAELI-PALESTINIAN LIAISON COMMITTEE

In order to provide for a smooth implementation of this Declaration of

Principles and any subsequent agreements pertaining to the interim period, upon the entry into force of this Declaration of Principles, a Joint Israeli-Palestinian Liaison Committee will be established in order to deal with issues requiring coordination, other issues of common interest and disputes.

Article XI

ISRAELI-PALESTINIAN COOPERATION IN ECONOMIC FIELDS

Recognizing the mutual benefit of cooperation in promoting the development of the West Bank, the Gaza Strip and Israel, upon the entry into force of this Declaration of Principles, an Israeli-Palestinian Economic Cooperation Committee will be established in order to develop and implement in a cooperative manner the programmes identified in the protocols attached as Annex III and Annex IV.

Article XII

LIAISON AND COOPERATION WITH JORDAN AND EGYPT

The two parties will invite the Governments of Jordan and Egypt to participate in establishing further liaison and cooperation arrangements between the Government of Israel and the Palestinian representatives, on the one hand, and the Governments of Jordan and Egypt, on the other hand, to promote cooperation between them. These arrangements will include the constitution of a Continuing Committee that will decide by agreement on the modalities of admission of persons displaced from the West Bank and Gaza Strip in 1967, together with necessary measures to prevent disruption and disorder. Other matters of common concern will be dealt with by this Committee.

Article XIII

REDEPLOYMENT OF ISRAELI FORCES

1. After the entry into force of this Declaration of Principles, and not later than the eve of elections for the Council, a redeployment of Israeli military forces in the West Bank and the Gaza Strip will take place, in

addition to withdrawal of Israeli forces carried out in accordance with Article XIV.

2. In redeploying its military forces, Israel will be guided by the principle that its military forces should be redeployed outside populated areas.

3. Further redeployments to specified locations will be gradually implemented commensurate with the assumption of responsibility for public order and internal security by the Palestinian police force pursuant to Article VIII above.

Article XIV

ISRAELI WITHDRAWAL FROM THE GAZA STRIP AND JERICHO AREA

Israel will withdraw from the Gaza Strip and Jericho area, as detailed in the protocol attached as Annex II.

Article XV

RESOLUTION OF DISPUTES

1. Disputes arising out of the application or interpretation of this Declaration of Principles, or any subsequent agreements pertaining to the interim period, shall be resolved by negotiations through the Joint Liaison Committee to be established pursuant to Article X above.

2. Disputes which cannot be settled by negotiations may be resolved by a mechanism of conciliation to be agreed upon by the parties.

3. The parties may agree to submit to arbitration disputes relating to the interim period, which cannot be settled through conciliation. To this end, upon the agreement of both parties, the parties will establish an Arbitration Committee.

Article XVI

ISRAELI-PALESTINIAN COOPERATION CONCERNING REGIONAL PROGRAMMES

Both parties view the multilateral working groups as an appropriate instrument for promoting a "Marshall Plan", the regional programmes and other programmes, including special programmes for the West Bank and Gaza Strip, as indicated in the protocol attached as Annex IV.

Article XVII

MISCELLANEOUS PROVISIONS

1. This Declaration of Principles will enter into force one month after its signing.

2. All protocols annexed to this Declaration of Principles and Agreed Minutes pertaining thereto shall be regarded as an integral part hereof.

DONE at Washington, D.C., this thirteenth day of September 1993.

For the Government of Israel:

For the PLO:

(Signed) Shimon PERES

(Signed) Mahmud ABBAS

Witnessed By:

The United States of America:

The Russian Federation:

(Signed) Warren CHRISTOPHER

(Signed) Andrei V. KOZYREV

ANNEX I

Protocol on the Mode and Conditions of Elections

1. Palestinians of Jerusalem who live there will have the right to participate in the election process, according to an agreement between the two sides.

2. In addition, the election agreement should cover, among other things, the following issues:

(a) The system of elections;

(b) The mode of the agreed supervision and international observation and their personal composition;

(c) Rules and regulations regarding election campaigns, including agreed arrangements for the organizing of mass media, and the possibility of licensing a broadcasting and television station.

3. The future status of displaced Palestinians who were registered on 4 June 1967 will not be prejudiced because they are unable to participate in the election process owing to practical reasons.

ANNEX II

Protocol on Withdrawal of Israeli Forces from the Gaza Strip and Jericho Area

1. The two sides will conclude and sign within two months from the date of entry into force of this Declaration of Principles an agreement on the withdrawal of Israeli military forces from the Gaza Strip and Jericho area. This agreement will include comprehensive arrangements to apply in the Gaza Strip and the Jericho area subsequent to the Israeli withdrawal.

2. Israel will implement an accelerated and scheduled withdrawal of Israeli military forces from the Gaza Strip and Jericho area, beginning immediately with the signing of the agreement on the Gaza Strip and Jericho area and to be completed within a period not exceeding four months after the signing of this agreement.

3. The above agreement will include, among other things:

(a) Arrangements for a smooth and peaceful transfer of authority from the Israeli military government and its Civil Administration to the Palestinian representatives;

(b) Structure, powers and responsibilities of the Palestinian authority in these areas, except: external security, settlements, Israelis, foreign relations and other mutually agreed matters;

(c) Arrangements for the assumption of internal security and public order by the Palestinian police force consisting of police officers recruited locally and from abroad (holding Jordanian passports and Palestinian documents issued by Egypt). Those who will participate in the Palestinian police force coming from abroad should be trained as police and police officers;

(d) A temporary international or foreign presence, as agreed upon;

(e) Establishment of a joint Palestinian-Israeli Coordination and Cooperation Committee for mutual security purposes;

(f) An economic development and stabilization programme including the establishment of an Emergency Fund, to encourage foreign investment and financial and economic support. Both sides will coordinate and cooperate jointly and unilaterally with regional and international parties to support these aims;

(g) Arrangements for a safe passage for persons and transportation between the Gaza Strip and Jericho area.

4. The above agreement will include arrangements for coordination between both parties regarding passages:

(a) Gaza - Egypt;

(b) Jericho - Jordan.

5. The offices responsible for carrying out the powers and responsibilities of the Palestinian authority under this Annex II and Article VI of the Declaration of Principles will be located in the Gaza Strip and in the Jericho area pending the inauguration of the Council.

6. Other than these agreed arrangements, the status of the Gaza Strip and Jericho area will continue to be an integral part of the West Bank and Gaza Strip, and will not be changed in the interim period.

ANNEX III

Protocol on Israeli-Palestinian Cooperation
in Economic and Development Programmes

The two sides agree to establish an Israeli-Palestinian Continuing Committee for Economic Cooperation, focusing, among other things, on the following:

1. Cooperation in the field of water, including a Water Development Programme prepared by experts from both sides, which will also specify the mode of cooperation in the management of water resources in the West Bank and Gaza Strip, and will include proposals for studies and plans on water rights of each party, as well as on the equitable utilization of joint water resources for implementation in and beyond the interim period.

2. Cooperation in the field of electricity, including an Electricity Development Programme, which will also specify the mode of cooperation for the production, maintenance, purchase and sale of electricity resources.

3. Cooperation in the field of energy, including an Energy Development Programme, which will provide for the exploitation of oil and gas for industrial purposes, particularly in the Gaza Strip and in the Negev, and will encourage further joint exploitation of other energy resources. This Programme may also provide for the construction of a petrochemical industrial complex in the Gaza Strip and the construction of oil and gas pipelines.

4. Cooperation in the field of finance, including a Financial Development and Action Programme for the encouragement of international investment in the West Bank and the Gaza Strip, and in Israel, as well as the establishment of a Palestinian Development Bank.

5. Cooperation in the field of transport and communications, including a Programme, which will define guidelines for the establishment of a Gaza Sea Port Area, and will provide for the establishing of transport and communications lines to and from the West Bank and the Gaza Strip to Israel and to other countries. In addition, this Programme will provide for carrying out the necessary construction of roads, railways, communications lines, etc.

6. Cooperation in the field of trade, including studies, and Trade Promotion Programmes, which will encourage local, regional and interregional trade, as well as a feasibility study of creating free trade zones in the Gaza Strip and in Israel, mutual access to these zones and cooperation in other areas related to trade and commerce.

7. Cooperation in the field of industry, including Industrial Development Programmes, which will provide for the establishment of joint Israeli-Palestinian Industrial Research and Development Centres, will promote Palestinian-Israeli joint ventures, and provide guidelines for cooperation in the textile, food, pharmaceutical, electronics, diamonds, computer and science-based industries.

8. A Programme for cooperation in, and regulation of, labour relations and cooperation in social welfare issues.

9. A Human Resource Development and Cooperation Plan, providing for joint Israeli-Palestinian workshops and seminars, and for the establishment of joint vocational training centres, research institutes and data banks.

10. An Environmental Protection Plan, providing for joint and/or coordinated measures in this sphere.

11. A Programme for developing coordination and cooperation in the field of communications and media.

12. Any other programmes of mutual interest.

ANNEX IV

Protocol on Israeli-Palestinian Cooperation concerning Regional Development Programmes

1. The two sides will cooperate in the context of the multilateral peace efforts in promoting a Development Programme for the region, including the West Bank and the Gaza Strip, to be initiated by the Group of Seven. The parties will request the Group of Seven to seek the participation in this Programme of other interested States, such as members of the Organisation for Economic Cooperation and Development, regional Arab States and institutions, as well as members of the private sector.

2. The Development Programme will consist of two elements:

(a) An Economic Development Programme for the West Bank and the Gaza Strip;

(b) A Regional Economic Development Programme.

A. The Economic Development Programme for the West Bank and the Gaza Strip will consist of the following elements:

(1) A Social Rehabilitation Programme, including a Housing and Construction Programme;

(2) A Small and Medium Business Development Plan;

(3) An Infrastructure Development Programme (water, electricity, transportation and communications, etc.);

(4) A Human Resources Plan;

(5) Other programmes.

B. The Regional Economic Development Programme may consist of the following elements:

(1) The establishment of a Middle East Development Fund, as a first step, and a Middle East Development Bank, as a second step;

(2) The development of a joint Israeli-Palestinian-Jordanian Plan for coordinated exploitation of the Dead Sea area;

(3) The Mediterranean Sea (Gaza) - Dead Sea Canal;

(4) Regional desalinization and other water development projects;
(5) A regional plan for agricultural development, including a coordinated regional effort for the prevention of desertification;

(6) Interconnection of electricity grids;

(7) Regional cooperation for the transfer, distribution and industrial exploitation of gas, oil and other energy resources;

(8) A Regional Tourism, Transportation and Telecommunications Development Plan;

(9) Regional cooperation in other spheres.

3. The two sides will encourage the multilateral working groups and will coordinate towards their success. The two parties will encourage inter-sessional activities, as well as pre-feasibility and feasibility studies, within the various multilateral working groups.

Agreed Minutes to the Declaration of Principles on Interim Self-Government Arrangements

A. GENERAL UNDERSTANDINGS AND AGREEMENTS

Any powers and responsibilities transferred to the Palestinians pursuant to the Declaration of Principles prior to the inauguration of the Council will be subject to the same principles pertaining to Article IV, as set out in these Agreed Minutes below.

B. SPECIFIC UNDERSTANDINGS AND AGREEMENTS

Article IV

It is understood that:

1. Jurisdiction of the Council will cover West Bank and Gaza Strip territory, except for issues that will be negotiated in the permanent status negotiations: Jerusalem, settlements, military locations and Israelis.

2. The Council's jurisdiction will apply with regard to the agreed powers, responsibilities, spheres and authorities transferred to it.

Article VI (2)

It is agreed that the transfer of authority will be as follows:

1. The Palestinian side will inform the Israeli side of the names of the authorized Palestinians who will assume the powers, authorities and responsibilities that will be transferred to the Palestinians according to the Declaration of Principles in the following fields: education and culture, health, social welfare, direct taxation, tourism and any other authorities agreed upon.

2. It is understood that the rights and obligations of these offices will not be affected.

3. Each of the spheres described above will continue to enjoy existing budgetary allocations in accordance with arrangements to be mutually agreed upon. These arrangements also will provide for the necessary adjustments required in order to take into account the taxes collected by the direct taxation office.

4. Upon the execution of the Declaration of Principles, the Israeli and Palestinian delegations will immediately commence negotiations on a detailed plan for the transfer of authority on the above offices in accordance with the above understandings.

Article VII (2)

The Interim Agreement will also include arrangements for coordination and cooperation.

Article VII (5)

The withdrawal of the military government will not prevent Israel from exercising the powers and responsibilities not transferred to the Council.

Article VIII

It is understood that the Interim Agreement will include arrangements for cooperation and coordination between the two parties in this regard. It is also agreed that the transfer of powers and responsibilities to the Palestinian police will be accomplished in a phased manner, as agreed in the Interim Agreement.

Article X

It is agreed that, upon the entry into force of the Declaration of Principles, the Israeli and Palestinian delegations will exchange the names of the individuals designated by them as members of the Joint Israeli-Palestinian Liaison Committee. It is further agreed that each side will have an equal number of members in the Joint Committee. The Joint Committee will reach decisions by agreement. The Joint Committee may add other technicians and experts, as necessary. The Joint Committee will decide on the frequency and place or places of its meetings.

ANNEX II

It is understood that, subsequent to the Israeli withdrawal, Israel will continue to be responsible for external security, and for internal security and public order of settlements and Israelis. Israeli military forces and civilians may continue to use roads freely within the Gaza Strip and the Jericho area.

DONE at Washington, D.C., this thirteenth day of September 1993.

For the Government of Israel:	For the PLO:
(Signed) Shimon PERES	(Signed) Mahmud ABBAS

Witnessed By:

The United States of America:	The Russian Federation:
(Signed) Warren CHRISTOPHER	(Signed) Andrei V. KOZYREV

Appendix K

United Nations Security Council Resolution 1397, 2002

<u>SECURITY COUNCIL DEMANDS</u>

<u>IMMEDIATE CESSATION OF ALL</u>

<u>VIOLENCE IN MIDDLE EAST;</u>

<u>AFFIRMS VISION OF TWO STATES,</u>

<u>ISRAEL AND PALESTINE</u>

"The Security Council,

"Recalling all its previous relevant resolutions, in particular resolutions 242 (1967) and 338 (1973),

"Affirming a vision of a region where two States, Israel and Palestine, live side by side within secure and recognized borders,

"Expressing its grave concern at the continuation of the tragic and violent events that have taken place since September 2000, especially the recent attacks and the increased number of casualties,

"Stressing the need for all concerned to ensure the safety of civilians,

"Stressing also the need to respect the universally accepted norms of international humanitarian law,

"Welcoming and encouraging the diplomatic efforts of special envoys from the United States of America, the Russian Federation, the

European Union and the United Nations Special Coordinator and others to bring about a comprehensive, just and lasting peace in the Middle East,

"Welcoming the contribution of Saudi Crown Prince Abdullah,

"1.   *Demands* immediate cessation of all acts of violence, including all acts of terror, provocation, incitement and destruction;

"2.   *Calls upon* the Israeli and Palestinian sides and their leaders to cooperate in the implementation of the Tenet work plan and Mitchell Report recommendations with the aim of resuming negotiations on a political settlement;

"3.   *Expresses* support for the efforts of the Secretary-General and others to assist the parties to halt the violence and to resume the peace process;

"4.   *Decides* to remain seized of the matter."

Adopted by vote of 14 in favour to none
against, with 1 Abstention

Appendix L
(i)
"Road Map", July 2002

"Quartet" Joint Statement

Following is the text of a joint statement issued by the "Quartet" (United Nations, Russian Federation, the United States and the European Union) following their meeting in New York.

United Nations Secretary-General Kofi Annan, Russian Foreign Minister Igor Ivanov, U.S. Secretary of State Colin L. Powell, Danish Foreign Minister Per Stig Moeller, High Representative for European Common Foreign and Security Policy Javier Solana and European Commissioner for External Affairs Chris Patten met in New York today. The Quartet members reviewed the situation in the Middle East and agreed to continue close consultations, as expressed in the Madrid Declaration, to which the Quartet remains fully committed, to promote a just, comprehensive, and lasting settlement of the Middle East conflict. The Quartet expresses its support for the convening of a further international Ministerial meeting at an appropriate time.

The Quartet deeply deplores today's tragic killing of Israeli civilians and reiterates its strong and unequivocal condemnation of terrorism, including suicide bombing, which is morally repugnant and has caused great harm to the legitimate aspirations of the Palestinian people for a better future. Terrorists must not be allowed to kill the hope of an entire region, and a united international community, for genuine peace and security for both Palestinians and Israelis. The Quartet expresses once again its profound regret at the loss of innocent Israeli and Palestinian lives, and extends its sympathy to all those who have suffered loss. The Quartet members expressed their increasing concern about the mounting humanitarian crisis in Palestinian areas and their determination to address urgent Palestinian needs.

Consistent with President Bush's June 24 statement, the UN, EU and

Russia express their strong support for the goal of achieving a final Israeli-Palestinian settlement which, with intensive effort on security and reform by all, could be reached within three years from now. The UN, EU and Russia welcome President Bush's commitment to active U.S. leadership toward that goal. The Quartet remains committed to implementing the vision of two states, Israel and an independent, viable and democratic Palestine, living side by side in peace and security, as affirmed by UN Security Council Resolution 1397. The Quartet members, in their individual capacity and jointly, pledge all possible efforts to realize the goals of reform, security and peace and reaffirm that progress in the political, security, economic, humanitarian, and institution-building fields must proceed together, hand-in-hand. The Quartet reiterates its welcome of the initiative of Saudi Arabia, endorsed by the Arab League Beirut Summit, as a significant contribution towards a comprehensive peace.

To assist progress toward these shared goals, the Quartet agreed on the importance of a coordinated international campaign to support Palestinian efforts at political and economic reform. The Quartet welcomes and encourages the strong Palestinian interest in fundamental reform, including the Palestinian 100-Day Reform Program. It also welcomes the willingness of regional states and the international community to assist the Palestinians to build institutions of good government, and to create a new governing framework of working democracy, in preparation for statehood. For these objectives to be realized, it is essential that well-prepared, free, open and democratic elections take place. The new international Task Force on Reform, which is comprised of representatives of the U.S., EU, UN Secretary General, Russia, Japan, Norway, the World Bank and the International Monetary Fund, and which works under the auspices of the Quartet, will strive to develop and implement a comprehensive action plan for reform. The inaugural meeting of this Task Force in London July 10 discussed a detailed plan including specific Palestinian commitments. It will meet again in August to review actions in areas including civil society, financial accountability, local government, the market economy, elections, and judicial and administrative reform.

Implementation of an action plan, with appropriate benchmarks for progress on reform measures, should lead to the establishment of a democratic Palestinian state characterized by the rule of law, separation of powers, and a vibrant free market economy that can best serve the interests of its people. The Quartet also commits itself to continuing to assist the parties in efforts to renew dialogue, and welcomes in this regard the recent high-level ministerial meetings between Israelis and Palestinians on the issues of security, economics and reform.

The Quartet agreed on the critical need to build new and efficient Palestinian security capabilities on sound bases of unified command, and transparency and accountability with regard to resources and conduct. Restructuring security institutions to serve these goals should lead to improvement in Palestinian security performance, which is essential to progress on other aspects of institutional transformation and realization of a Palestinian state committed to combating terror.

In this context, the Quartet notes Israel's vital stake in the success of Palestinian reform. The Quartet calls upon Israel to take concrete steps to support the emergence of a viable Palestinian state. Recognizing Israel's legitimate security concerns, these steps include immediate measures to ease the internal closures in certain areas and, as security improves through reciprocal steps, withdrawal of Israeli forces to their pre-September 28, 2000 positions. Moreover, frozen tax revenues should be released. In this connection, a more transparent and accountable mechanism is being put into place. In addition, consistent with the Mitchell Committee's recommendations, Israel should stop all new settlement activity. Israel must also ensure full, safe and unfettered access for international and humanitarian personnel.

The Quartet reaffirms that there must be a negotiated permanent settlement based on UN Security Council resolutions 242 and 338. There can be no military solution to the conflict; Israelis and Palestinians must address the core issues that divide them, through sustained negotiations, if there is to be real and lasting peace and security. The Israeli occupation that began in 1967 must end, and Israel must have secure and recognized borders. The Quartet further reaffirms its commitment to the goal of a comprehensive regional peace between Israel and Lebanon, and Israel and Syria, based upon Resolutions 242 and 338, the Madrid terms of reference, and the principle of land for peace.

The Quartet looks forward to upcoming consultations with the Foreign Ministers of Jordan, Egypt, Saudi Arabia, and other regional partners, and determines to continue regular consultation on the situation in the

Middle East at the principals' level. The Quartet envoys will continue their work on the ground to support the work of the principals, to assist the Task Force on Reform, and to aid the parties in resuming a political dialogue in order to reach a solution to the core political questions.

(ii)

"Road Map", 2003

The following is a performance-based and goal driven roadmap, with clear phases, timelines, target dates, and benchmarks aiming at progress through reciprocal steps by the two parties in the political, security, economic, humanitarian, and institution-building fields, under the auspices of the Quartet. The destination is a final and comprehensive settlement of the Israel-Palestinian conflict by 2005, as presented in President Bush's speech of 24 June, and welcomed by the EU, Russia, and the UN in the 16 July and 17 September Quartet Ministerial statements.

A two state solution to the Israeli-Palestinian conflict will only be achieved through an end to violence and terrorism, when the Palestinian people have a leadership acting decisively against terror and willing able to build a practicing democracy based on tolerance and liberty, and through Israeli's readiness to do what is necessary for a democratic Palestinian state to be established, and a clear, unambiguous acceptance by both parties of the goal of a negotiated settlement as described below. The Quartet will assist and facilitate implementation of the plan, starting in Phase I, including direct discussions between the parties as required. The plan establishes a realistic timeline for implementation. However, as a performance-based plan, progress will require and depend upon the good faith efforts of the parties, and their compliance with each of the obligations outlined below. Should the parties perform their obligations rapidly, progress within and through the phases may come sooner than indicated in the plan. Non-compliance with obligations will impede progress.

A settlement, negotiated between the parties, will result in the emergence of an independent, democratic, and viable Palestinian state living side by side in peace and security with Israel and its other neighbors. The settlement will resolve the Israel-Palestinian conflict, and end the occupation that began in 1967, based on the foundations on the Madrid Conference, the principle of land for peace, UNSCRs

242, 338 and 1397, agreements previously reached by the parties, and the initiative of Saudi Crown Prince Abdullah - endorsed by the Beirut Arab League Summit - calling for acceptance of Israel as a neighbor living in peace and security, in the context of a comprehensive settlement. This initiative is a vital element of international efforts to promote a comprehensive peace on all tracks, including the Syrian-Israeli and Lebanese-Israeli tracks.

The Quartet will meet regularly at senior levels to evaluate the parties' performance on implementation of the plan. In each phase, the parties are expected t perform their obligations in parallel, unless otherwise indicated.

PHASE I: ENDING TERROR AND VIOLENCE, NORMALIZING PALESTINIAN LIFE, AND BUILDING PALESTINIAN INSTITUTIONS PRESENT TO MAY 2003

In Phase I. the Palestinians immediately undertake and unconditional cessation of violence according to the steps outlined below; such action should be accompanied by supportive measures undertaken by Israel. Palestinians and Israelis resume security cooperation based on the Tenet work plan to end violence, terrorism, and incitement through restructured and effective Palestinian security services. Palestinian undertake comprehensive political reform in preparation for statehood, including drafting a Palestinian constitution, and free, fair and open elections upon the basis of those measures. Israel takes all necessary steps to help normalize Palestinian life. Israel withdraws from Palestinian areas occupied from September 28, 2000 and the two sides restore the status quo that existed at that time, as security performance and cooperation progress. Israel also freezes all settlement activity, consistent with the Mitchell report.

At the outset of Phase I:

* Palestinian leadership issues unequivocal statement reiterating Israel's right to exist in peace and security and calling for an immediate and unconditional ceasefire to end armed activity and all acts of violence against Israelis anywhere. All official Palestinian institutions end incitement against Israel.

* Israeli leadership issues unequivocal statement affirming its

commitments to the two-state vision of an independent, viable, sovereign Palestinian state living in peace and security alongside Israel, as expressed by President Bush, and calling for an immediate end to violence against Palestinian everywhere. All official Israeli institutions end incitement against Palestinians.

Security
* Palestinians declare an unequivocal end to violence and terrorism and undertake visible efforts on the ground to arrest, disrupt, and restrain individuals and groups conduction and planning violent attacks on Israelis anywhere.

* Rebuilt and refocused Palestinian Authority security apparatus begins sustained, targeted, and effective operations aimed at confronting all those engaged in terror and dismantlement of terrorist capabilities and infrastructure. This includes commencing confiscation of illegal weapons and consolidation of security authority, free of association with terror and corruption.

* GOI takes no actions undermining trust, including deportations, attack on civilians; confiscation and/or demolition of Palestinian homes and property, as a punitive measure or to facilitate Israeli construction; destruction of Palestinian institutions and infrastructure; and other measures specified in the Tenet Work Plan.

* Relying on existing mechanisms and on-the ground resources, Quartet representatives begin informal monitoring and consult with the parties on establishment of a formal monitoring mechanism and its implementation.

*Implementation, as previously agreed, of U.S. rebuilding, training and resumed security cooperation plan in collaboration with outside oversight board (U.S. - Egypt - Jordan). Quartet support for efforts to achieve a lasting, comprehensive cease-fire.
* All Palestinian security organizations are consolidated into three services reporting to an empowered Interior Minister.

* Restructured/retained Palestinian security forces and IDF counterparts progressively resume security cooperation and other undertakings in implementation of the Tenet work plan, including regular senior-level meetings, with the participation of U.S. security officials.

* Arab states cut off public and private funding and all other forms of support for groups supporting and engaging in violence and terror.

* All donors providing budgetary support for the Palestinians channel these funds through the Palestinian Ministry of Finance's Single Treasury Account.
As comprehensive security performance moves forward, IDF withdraws progressively from areas occupied since September 28, 2000 and the two sides restore the status quo that existed prior to September 28, 2000. Palestinian security forces redeploy to areas vacated by IDF.

Palestinian Institution-building

* Immediate action on credible process to produce draft constitution for Palestinian statehood. As rapidly as possible, constitutional committee circulates draft Palestinian constitution, based on strong parliamentary democracy and cabinet with empowered prime minister, for public comment/debate. Constitutional committee proposes draft document for submission after elections for approval by appropriate Palestinian institutions.
* Appointment of interim prime minister or cabinet with empowered executive authority/decision-making body.

* GOI fully facilitates travel of Palestinian officials for PLC and Cabinet sessions, internationally supervised security retraining, electoral and other reform activity, and other supportive measures related to the reform efforts.

* Continued appointment of Palestinian ministers empowered to undertake fundamental reform. Completion of further steps to achieve genuine separation of powers, including any necessary Palestinian legal reforms for this purpose.

* Establishment of independent Palestinian election commission. PLC reviews and revises elections law.
Palestinian performance on judicial, administrative, and economic benchmarks, as established by the International Task Force on Palestinian Reform.

* As early as possible, and based upon the above measures and in the context of open debate and transparent candidate selection/electoral campaign based on a free, multiparty process, Palestinians hold free, open, and fair elections.

* GOI facilitates Task Force election assistance, registration of voters, movement of candidates and voting officials. Support for NGOs involved in the election process.

* GOI reopens Palestinian Chamber of Commerce and other closed Palestinian institutions in East Jerusalem based on a commitment that these institutions operate strictly in accordance with prior agreements between the parties.

Humanitarian Response

* Israel takes measures to improve the humanitarian situation. Israel and Palestinians implement in full all recommendations of the Bertini report to improve humanitarian conditions, lifting curfews, and easing restrictions on movement of persons and goods, and allowing full, safe, and unfettered access of international and humanitarian personnel.

* AHLC reviews the humanitarian situation and prospects for economic development in the West Bank and Gaza and launches a major donor assistance effort, including to the reform effort.

* GOI and PA continue revenue clearance process and transfer of funds, including arrears, in accordance with agreed, transparent monitoring mechanism.

Civil Society

* Continued donor support, including increased funding through PVOs/NGOs, for people to people programs, private sector development and civil society initiatives.

Settlements

* GOI immediately dismantles settlement outposts erected since March 2001.

* Consistent with the Mitchell Report, GOI freezes all settlement

activity (including natural growth of settlements).

PHASE II. TRANSITION JUNE 2003 - DECEMBER 2003

In the second phase, efforts are focused on the option of creating an independent Palestinian state with provisional borders and attributes of sovereignty, based on the new constitution, as a way station to a permanent status settlement. As has been noted, this goal can be achieved when the Palestinian people have a leadership acting decisively against terror, willing and able to build a practicing democracy based on tolerance and liberty. With such a leadership, reformed civil institutions and security structures, the Palestinians will have the active support of the Quartet and the broader international community in establishing an independent, viable, state.

Progress into Phase II will be based upon the consensus judgment of the Quartet of whether conditions are appropriate to proceed, taking into account performance of both parties. Furthering and sustaining efforts to normalize Palestinian lives and build Palestinian institutions, Phase II starts after Palestinian elections and ends with possible creation of an independent Palestinian state with provisional borders in 2003. Its primary goals are continued comprehensive security performance and effective security cooperation, continued normalization of Palestinian life and institution-building, further building on and sustaining of the goals outlined in Phase I, ratification of a democratic Palestinian constitution, formal establishment of office of prime minister, consolidation of political reform, and the creation of a Palestinian state with provisional borders.
INTERNATIONAL CONFERENCE: Convened by the Quartet, in consultation with the parties, immediately after the successful conclusion of Palestinian elections, to support Palestinian economic recovery and launch a process, leading to establishment of an independent Palestinian state with provisional borders.

* Such a meeting would be inclusive, based on the goal of a comprehensive Middle East peace (including between Israel and Syria, and Israel and Lebanon), and based on the principles described in the preamble to this document.

* Arab states restore pre-intifada links to Israel (trade offices, etc.).

* Revival of multilateral engagement on issues including regional water resources, environment, economic development, refugees, and arms control issues.

* New constitution for democratic, independent Palestinian state is finalized and approved by appropriate Palestinian institutions. Further elections, if required, should follow approval of the new constitution.

* Empowered reform cabinet with office of prime minister formally established, consistent with draft constitution.
Continued comprehensive security performance, including effective security cooperation on the bases laid out in Phase I.

* Creation of an independent Palestinian state with provisional borders through a process of Israeli-Palestinian engagement. Launched by the international conference. As part of this process, implementation of prior agreements, to enhance maximum territorial contiguity, including further action on settlements in conjunction with establishment of a Palestinian state with provisional borders.

* Enhanced international role in monitoring transition, with the active, sustained, and operational support of the Quartet.

* Quartet members promote international recognition of Palestinian state, including possible UN membership.

PHASE III: PERMANENT STATUS AGREEMENT AND END OF THE ISRAELI-PALESTINIAN CONFLICT 2004 - 2005

Progress into Phase III, based on consensus judgment of Quartet, and taking into account actions of both parties and Quartet monitoring. Phase III objectives are consolidation of reform and stabilization of Palestinian institutions, sustained, effective Palestinian security performance, and Israeli-Palestinian negotiations aimed at a permanent status agreement in 2005.

SECOND INTERNATIONAL CONFERENCE: Convened by Quartet, in consultation with the parties, at beginning of 2004 to endorse agreement reached on an independent Palestinian state with provisional borders and formally to launch a process with the active, sustained, and operational support of the Quartet, leading to a final, permanent status resolution in 2005, including on borders, Jerusalem, refugees, settlements; and, to support progress toward a comprehensive Middle East settlement between Israel and Lebanon and Israel and Syria, to be achieved as soon as possible.

* Continued comprehensive, effective progress on the reform agenda laid out by the Task Force in preparation for final status agreement. Continued sustained and effective security performance, and sustained, effective security cooperation on the basis laid out in Phase I. International efforts to facilitate reform and stabilize Palestinian institutions and the Palestinian economy, in preparation for final status agreement.

* Parties reach final and comprehensive permanent status agreement that ends the Israel - Palestinian conflict in 2005, through a settlement negotiated between the parties based on UNSCR 242, 338, and 1397, that ends the occupation that began in 1967, and includes an agreed, just, fair, and realistic solution to the refugee issue, and a negotiated resolution on the status of Jerusalem that takes into account the political and religious concerns of both sides, and protects the religious interests of Jews, Christians, and Muslims worldwide, and fulfills the vision of two states, Israel and sovereign, independent, democratic and viable Palestine, living side-by-side in peace and security.

* Arab state acceptance of full normal relations with Israel and security for all the states of the region in the context of a compressive Arab-Israeli peace.

Index